OPULENCE AND OSTENTATION

OPULENCE AND OSTENTATION

Building the Circus

Steve Ward, PhD

Modern Vaudeville Press

Opulence and Ostentation: Building the Circus / Steve Ward
Edited by Thom Wall
Cover photo by Kari Nieminen
Cover typography by Robin Gunney

Modern Vaudeville Press
113 E. Mayland St.
Philadelphia, PA 19144
USA
www.modernvaudevillepress.com
info@modernvaudevillepress.com

ISBN: 978-1-958604-02-1
Library of Congress: 2023906425

CONTENTS

ACKNOWLEDGEMENTS

In compiling this book, I have received help and support from many people and organisations. I would especially like to mention the following;

The British Library; The Leeds Library; The Art department of the Leeds City Library; the Linen Hall Library Belfast; the National Library of Norway; Gothenburg University Library; the Regional Archives Gothenburg; Stockholm University of the Arts; the University of Oslo Library; the Norwegian University of Science and Technology, Trondheim (NTNU); Oslo Museum Library; the University of Warsaw Library; the city of Sydney Archives; New York History Library and Archive; Free Library of Philadelphia; Bolshoi St. Petersburg State Circus, Museum of Circus Art; Emese Joó and David Konyöt of the Hungarian Circus Art Museum and Archive; Szandra Szolday (Hungary); Szabó Ádám (Hungary); Jamila Attou (CEDAC Verona); Antonio Giarola (Italy); Will Visconti (Australia); Olivia Ricken (New Zealand); Lolita Lipinska (Latvia); Jörgen Börsch (Denmark); Kari Nieminen (Finland); Simon Goldrick and Aine Dolan (Belfast); Gilles Maignant (France); David Fisher (Brighton); Thom Wall (USA); Paul Bouissac (Canada); Johanna Abrahamsson (Cirkusvarnen project); Lennart Strandner (Sweden); Megan Starr and Darmon Richter (for information on Soviet circuses); Caroline Palmer; Charlie Holland; Chris Barltrop – and finally, Linda, my 'circus widow' wife for her constant support and understanding.

FOREWORD: BOUISSAC

The circus is a nomadic art. Its magic is ephemeral and elusive. The spectacular acts it produces linger, magnified, in our imagination, but most of its wonders could hardly survive repeated examinations, day after day. Part skills, part illusions, they would soon lose their drama and their shine. For ages, it appeared suddenly on village squares and fairgrounds, and vanished as suddenly through untraceable itineraries. The perpetual motion from places to places is of the essence of the circus. It would seem that the notion of a stable circus is a paradox, if not an oxymoron.

However, in the wake of Philip Astley's London Amphitheatre, toward the end of the eighteenth century, buildings dedicated to the circus arts appeared in most European cities. Their munificence, often on par with opera houses, bears witness to the new popularity and cultural prestige of the circus. The urban demographic explosion caused by the industrial revolution created business opportunities both for circus families which had accumulated a significant capital and for entrepreneurs who sought to invest in the competitive but profitable market of popular entertainment. Dubbed the 'golden age' of the circus, the nineteenth century saw the construction of numerous permanent or semi-permanent premises designed to accommodate circus artists and their animals. Concurrently, monumental tenting shows kept roaming Europe and the Americas.

When new forms of mass entertainment caused the decline of the popularity of the circus, most of the dedicated buildings were demolished or recycled. This cultural erasure is an irrevocable loss. It is fortunate that eminent historian of the circus Dr. Steve Ward has endeavoured to document and analyse this trove of architectural treasures that reflected the cultural centrality of the circus arts for almost two centuries.

Paul Bouissac
Emeritus Professor, University of Toronto
Toronto, Canada

FOREWORD: KÖNYÖT

The first International Academic Conference on Circus Buildings was on 11 January 2022. The initial idea came from Péter Fekete, who at the time was the Hungarian Minister for Culture. Organising the event was undertaken by the Budapest Capital Circus and the Museum of Hungarian Circus Arts, with the first order of business to find experts in the field. Following the innovation of what is now widely regarded as 'Modern Circus' by Phillip Astley in 1768, construction of static circus buildings throughout Europe gathered pace and continued for over a century but unlike other great social advances there was very little academic interest and the circus community became the guardian of its own history.

Dr. Steve Ward was one of the exceptions to this state of affairs; his extensive, wide ranging knowledge of circus buildings, especially in the UK, assured that his name was one of the first on the list of contributors at the event. He was alone in finding evidence of long forgotten buildings in the UK, many of them temporary or destroyed but his excellent research and delivery brought them to life at the Conference.

Opulence and Ostentation takes a wider and more comprehensive look at the subject, encompassing not just Europe but North America and Australasia with a glance at Asia and the Far East, which promises to be a lucrative area for future research.

David Könyöt
Researcher at the Museum of Hungarian Circus Arts
Budapest, Hungary

FOREWORD: WARD

The circus is like Marmite; you either love it or you hate it. Me, I love it, can't get enough of it, I could probably overdose on it! But on whichever side of the fence you stand, it must be acknowledged that the circus has a long and colourful history.

Throughout my research into various aspects of the social and cultural history of the circus there is one fascinating phenomenon that has caught my particular interest; the circus building. During the latter half of the nineteenth century and into the twentieth century many circus owners, and indeed civic authorities, commissioned buildings specifically for circus. Why, you may ask, for such an ephemeral entertainment? I consider that this growth in circus building reflects the popularity of the art form at that time. Some of these buildings were vast cathedrals of circus and could accommodate thousands of people and were regularly filled to capacity. From early developments in Britain in the late eighteenth century, circus buildings were constructed across Europe; from Scandinavia in the north, Imperial Russia in the east, and south into Mediterranean countries. As global travel increased during the nineteenth century, circus buildings also began to appear in the United States of America and in Australasia.

The existing historic circus buildings that remain today are of stone, brick, or concrete. They were constructed for permanence. But not all permanent circus buildings were of such hardy material. Many circus buildings constructed of wood, or mixed materials, were intended at point of construction as permanent. Several lasted for many decades before being either demolished or redeveloped. To say that a permanent circus is only one which is built of stone is somewhat misleading and we should consider wooden structures that were intended for a prolonged use. In this work I have included examples of more permanent wooden circus buildings, as some of them were as opulent and ostentatious as their stone-built counterparts and an important part of the cultural heritage of the circus.

In my exploration of circus buildings there will be some that I have missed, I am sure. I apologise for this if you feel that there are buildings I should have mentioned. There will also be parts of the world that I have not covered. This has been a more conscious decision on my part, as research is ever ongoing and allows for future discoveries and publications. This book is not intended as a history of the circus, although by its very nature the subject is a part of that history. Neither is it intended as a catalogue of circus buildings, owners, and performers, although many are mentioned. It is my intention to show the wealth and breadth of this phase of circus development. For fans of the circus, I hope it will prove illuminating and provide an insight into an aspect of the circus that perhaps you know little about. For the general reader I hope that it will be interesting and informative.

Steve Ward
Leeds, England

INTRODUCTION

Circus requires two essential things; an audience and a space. Without these a circus is not a circus. Implicit within any performance art is the presence of an audience. The audience contextualises the performance within its defined space. An artistic performance becomes an interaction with the audience, it is an activity of communication (Brown, 2011 in Pitches & Popat (eds), 2011:184). Kavanagh (2013:5) captures this notion succinctly,

> To me, circus speaks most clearly when a performed physical action invokes a physiological response, causing my heart to race, my breath to stop, or my tears flow; if my emotional response comes from an intellectual place alone, it is not circus. But, if there is no room for my intellect to explore and touch new realms of possibility, then it isn't circus anymore either.

The performers and the, often hidden, production team of lighting, sound, and costume, (who all enhance the aesthetic quality of the performance) give form and meaning to the performed activity, and the audience may interact in several ways; applause, gasps, tears, cheering, etc. In discussing her life as an aerialist, Rebecca Truman sometimes had to perform without an audience. She writes (Truman, 2018:5):

> It was very hard to perform properly with no audience; we would just go through the motions, no adrenaline, no feedback, weird and flat.

Audience feedback is vital for the dynamics of a performance. It is not just the tangible audience response in terms of applause etc. but there is another level of response that is more difficult to quantify. In the theatre, the invisible fourth wall is a performance convention (Bell, 2008:203) that creates a distance between the active performers and the passive audience. In the circus, the physical structure of the ring, now conceptually a volume to be filled, allows the audience to surround the action. The circus has a three-dimensional quality (Radosavlević, 2012:20). The dynamic of the ring is, for me, fundamental to the audience experience. It is something that is rooted deep in human ancestry; it is a natural space for people to gather (Jacob, 2018:9.) Early people gathered around a fire or a hearth. Primarily for warmth, yes, but also to share; to share stories, dances, rituals, and other activities. Even today it is natural to gather in a circle (or semi-circle) to watch performances of all kinds, witness the street performer marking out a performance area as the audience 'gathers around'. The ring allows for a sense of communion. Not only can the audience see the performers, but they can also see each other. This becomes a communal experience that can transform the [theatrically] passive audience into one that is revitalised and re-activated through the energy of the performance (Rancière, 2009:3). It could be argued that the circus provides a re-enchantment in a 'disenchanted' modern world; a world where the qualities of mystery and richness have been lost to scientific rationalisation (Jenkins, 2000:5).

At a Circus250 organised public Panel Discussion entitled *The Big Top across Five Continents – 250 years of Circus Worldwide* held in Sheffield on August 14 2018, Pascal Jacob, circus director and researcher of circus history, commented that for him the circle [ring] was an artistically organic form that allowed a sharing of an experience for everyone at the same moment. It is a space within which actions become more easily understood (Jacob, 2018 ibid.). Coxe (1951:17) touches on this when he talks about the audience response being an intensified emotion that 'runs around the arena like an electric current'. Hoak (2021:29) echoes this when she writes 'Watching circus is participatory. Spectator bodies are fully, physically invested in the performed actions'. It is a collective empathy that stretches between audience and performer; at the point where the audience become more than on-lookers and enter your world. But that world is both real and illusory at the same time. The circus embraces both elements. They are not diametrically opposed, and one does not necessarily exclude the other. They can be complementary. The audience knows that what they see, in terms of the physical actions presented, is real but when they enter the circus space, they accept that they are entering a world of the other; different from the reality of everyday experience, something beyond the norm. Through its practices and traditions, the circus has developed a culture of its own. It is a world of the exotic, disorder, inversion, and anomaly (Stoddard, 2000:89-90). The circus has consciously perpetuated this 'otherness' throughout its history. Examine circus advertising and you will often find adjectives such as exotic, beautiful, unrivalled, novel, antipodean, dangerous etc. This all adds to the idea of the otherness of the circus and as escapism from the ordinariness of everyday life for the audience.

The otherness of the circus is contained within that ring. Early performances were given in the open air, with the audience gathered around a demarcated area. Later in the development of the circus, performances were given within temporary wooden structures and then canvas tents. All of these allowed the circus to maintain its itinerant nature; arriving in a town, setting up a seemingly magical 'space out of place' (Bouissac, 2022), and then moving on again within a short period of time. It is far too simplistic to say that the development of the circus space into a permanent structure is linear; from open air, temporary wooden structures, portable canvas tents, semi-permanent wooden structures, and then stone built circuses. The varying structures co-existed for many years, until such time as the American creation of the 'big-top' became synonymous with circus and regularly adopted world-wide. But during the nineteenth century, and particularly the latter part of the century, there was a wave of civic building that caused many opulent and ostentatious static circus buildings (and conversions) to be built across Europe, and beyond. Although these buildings may have been intended to be permanent homes for the circus, and for me it is that intentionality of build that signifies permanence – not just the material used – the circus itself is intrinsically nomadic and therefore many (but not all) companies based in such buildings tended to tour during the summer months, wintering in their circus buildings. However, once circus venues became more permanent there were official records of them, unlike the earlier transient venues where we rely largely on ephemeral advertising and newspaper comments to evidence their existence. A few of these buildings still exist today as circus venues. Some still exist but have been repurposed, and many others have long since disappeared. The main period of circus building fell in the 100 years from 1850 to 1950, with a few exceptions beyond these parameters. I would now like to take you on a journey to explore some of the more significant circus buildings of the period.

A Village Fair. Pieter Brueghel the Younger (Public domain image)

CHAPTER 1

THE FOUNDATIONS

When considering the development of the defined circus performance space it is difficult not to mention Philip Astley. His demonstrations of horsemanship at his riding school, given at Halfpenny Hatch on the south bank of the river Thames in London in the spring of 1768 are considered to be the founding moment of the 'modern' circus. But Philip Astley did not invent the circus. Generic physical skills had been in existence for thousands of years before his time. The origins of many of these will never be known. Many of these skills will have had their origins in practical needs. We do not know who was the first person to balance across a thin rope or to walk upon stilts or to manipulate objects in time and space and begin to juggle, or more importantly why.

Pre-Astleian performers were largely itinerant, unless retained by the nobility for their own entertainment. They performed where they could, at fairs and markets, and anywhere a crowd might gather, such as in the seventeenth century painting by Pieter Brueghel the Younger, *A Village Fair*.

This tradition of the itinerant performer continued throughout the medieval period. They appeared under a variety of names from the ninth to the seventeenth centuries; jongleurs, gleemen, troubadours, and jesters. These would be adept in a variety of skills; acrobatics, tumbling, juggling, legerdemain, animal training, and foolery. Sometimes they were skilled in music and song as well. One unidentified jongleur is referred to by Speaight (1980) who described his ability to sing a song well, and make tales to please young ladies. He could throw knives into the air and catch them without cutting his fingers. He could balance chairs and make tables dance; could somersault and walk upon his hands.

By the middle of the seventeenth century things were to change drastically for itinerant performers throughout England. With the ending of the English Civil War and the execution of Charles I, the English Commonwealth was established under the control of Oliver Cromwell. During the period of the Interregnum, from 1649 – 1660, performances of dancing and plays by live actors were forbidden but the state did not challenge performances by puppets or other entertainers such as the jongleur and the rope-dancer. It is a little-known fact that Cromwell himself had in his service at least four 'buffoons'. All the skills of the jesters and other itinerant performers endured chiefly because of their popular nature. They were, and still are, entertainments of the people and people still needed to be entertained during those turbulent times. They survived in gatherings such as borough fairs; Bartholomew Fair, Southwark Fair and other May Fair gatherings.

William Hogarth gives us a vivid picture of what a borough fair would have looked like in his 1733 engraving *Southwark Fair or The Humours of a Fair.*

Southwark Fair. William Hogarth (Public domain image)

A multitude of people takes in the amusements and entertainments all around. People are pushing and shoving in their efforts to see what is going on. In the middle of the square is a very pretty woman playing a drum, accompanied by a small black boy on a trumpet. Above and behind them a man performs tricks on a slack rope slung between two buildings. This man is well-known as Violante. Between the church tower and a nearby tree another aerial performer called Cadman, known as the 'flying man', has stretched a rope. With his arms outstretched he descends the rope headfirst. Placards advertising forthcoming entertainments are all around. Behind the rope-dancer is one advertising Maximillian Muller, the famous German Giant, who is reputed to have stood over eight feet tall. On the right of the square another placard shows two contortionists. Beneath that placard on a balcony is a drumming monkey accompanying the famous Isaac Fawkes, a noted juggler and magician of the period. He is demonstrating a magic trick to the crowd. A dwarf drummer leads a man upon a horse. The man is holding a fearsome looking sword in his hand and I imagine that he will be giving a demonstration of swordsmanship later. Behind the gamblers and near a blind piper with his puppets, there is a dancing dog. Complete with hat, sword and cane, he is a very miniature of the gallants in the crowd. To the left of the picture a balcony collapses. These temporary booths were quite often thrown up very quickly just for the fairs and were not at all well-constructed. Men and women begin to tumble to the ground onto the heads of those below, as a small monkey clings desperately to one of the uprights. In his detailed engraving, Hogarth has given us what must have been a bustling, chaotic assault on the senses.

By the turn of the seventeenth century these markets had become less focused on business and increasingly more for pleasure, with a myriad of entertainments and now lasted for up to four weeks. Diarists such as John Evelyn and Samuel Pepys both visited Southwark Fair and commented on the sights to be seen. Evelyn describes seeing monkeys and asses dancing on a tightrope. He observed an Italian girl dance and perform tricks on the tightrope to much admiration, so much so that the whole Court went to see her. Another interesting exhibition that he saw, which could be taken directly from a modern circus, was that of a strong man who lifted up a piece of an iron cannon weighing about 400 pounds using only the hair of his head. In 1668 Samuel Pepys, in his diary[1], referred to visiting a 'very dirty' Southwark Fair, where he went to see Jacob Hall dancing on the rope.

... to visit the mare that tells money and many things to admire – and then the dancing ropes...and so to Jacob Hall's dancing of the ropes; a thing worth seeing, and mightily followed...

Pleasure Gardens were an early eighteenth-century development and continued through the nineteenth century. Oases of rural idyll, these gardens became places of entertainment and pleasure; art works were displayed in pavilions and music was played. In June 1764 even an eight-year-old Mozart gave a performance on the harpsichord in Chelsea's Ranalegh Gardens. Masquerades were always popular and recitals were given, very often accompanied by firework displays later in the century. But the gardens now also became venues for performers of physical feats. It was quite common for visitors strolling around the gardens to come across jugglers and acrobats. In Marylebone Gardens in 1738, a tall tower was erected so that a performer could walk across a stretched rope with a wheelbarrow, something that Blondin was to do much later when he famously crossed Niagara Falls. As early as the late seventeenth century, at the gardens on the site of the present-day Sadler's Wells theatre, rope-dancers were engaged to entertain the public.

Some of these activities moved into indoor venues as a network of minor theatres grew across the country. In the new Sadler's Wells theatre, performances of physical skills now took place inside the building. Between 1750 and 1800 there are several recorded performances of what we might term circus-style entertainments. Michael Maddox performed wire-dancing and 'tricks with a long straw'. In 1768 a Mister Spinacutti and his performing monkey made an appearance. There were tumblers such as Paul Redigé, also known as the 'Little Devil', and another named Placido; the Bologna and sons' act of feats of strength, and Costello with his performing dogs. Smollett, in his 1771 work *The Expedition of Humphrey Clinker* has the maid Winifred Jenkins give a very vivid description of a visit to Sadler's Wells:

I was afterwards at a party at Sadler's Wells where I saw such tumbling and dancing on ropes and wires that I was frightened and ready to go into a fit – I tho't it all inchantment [sic]; and believing myself bewitched, began to cry.

Similarly in Dublin, in the year 1727, a Madame Violante (possibly related to the Violante seen in Hogarth's print) engaged an extensive building, formerly occupied by Lord Chief Justice Whitchel, which she opened with a company of acrobats and rope-dancers[2]. After a time, these amusements ceased to attract, and she converted the building into a theatre, for the representation of plays and farces.

Throughout the eighteenth century and into the early nineteenth century physical performance skills not only survived but developed as highly popular forms of entertainment, supported by all classes of society. They took place in a wide variety of venues, from borough fairs to Pleasure Gardens to the London stage. The circus, as we might recognise it today, was about to be born and it would take one man to pull it all together and develop the idea of a specific performance genre, before a paying audience, and in a dedicated space with controlled entry. That man was Philip Astley.

Astley's first venue was little more than an open space, surrounded by fences and hoardings to prevent non-payers from watching the exhibitions.

A view of Astley's performance space at Halfpenny Hatch c. 1770

(Engraving published in Old and New London. *E.Walford 1878)*

Earlier exhibitions of horsemanship by the likes of Mr. Johnson in the grounds of Dobney's Inn in Islington were presented in a circular arena surrounded by seats or booths. Here, a hat was passed around and people contributed or not as they wished, much like street performers of today. Astley, however, controlled the entrance to his venture and anyone wanting to see his exhibitions of horsemanship had to pay. Performing with his wife and infant son, he presented demonstrations of *haute école*, military, and trick riding. Kwint (1994) suggests that each show could last for up to two hours. It was not long before Astley was introducing more novelty and narrative equestrian acts. The first was his 'Little Learned Horse' named Billy. Willson Disher (1937) gives a description of it. The horse would lie as if dead in the middle of the arena and Astley would commence his prologue:

> My horse lies dead, apparent at your sight,
> But I am the man who can set things to right,
> Speak when you please, I am ready to obey,
> My faithful horse knows what I want to say,
> But first pray give me leave to move his foot.
> That he is dead is quite beyond dispute.

At this point Astley would lift the leg of the horse, which would not react at all. He would then continue in his loud and commanding Sergeant Major's voice:

> This shows how brutes by heaven were designed
> To be in full subjection to mankind.
> Rise, young Bill, and be a little handy,
> To serve that warlike hero Granby.

And at this point the horse would rise to its feet with no obvious command from its master. To conclude, Astley would then turn to his audience and announce:

> When you have seen, all my bills expressed
> My wife, to conclude, performs the rest.

He would then lead off Little Billy to thunderous applause as his wife Patty entered the arena to conclude the show with a display of her own trick-riding – standing on her head, also firing a pistol whilst balancing on two horses.

The sketch *The Tailor Riding to Brentford* was another of Astley's interpretations of a popular act that he developed and presented. The act had its origins in the volatile political upheavals of the times. *The Tailor Riding to Brentford* was based on the fanciful exploits of a tailor who was desperate to get to the elections in time to vote for John Wilkes, a radical member of Parliament. Being an inept horseman, it allowed for all sorts of comic slap-stick gags to be woven into Astley's equestrian act. Astley took the character and named him *Billy Buttons*, and in doing so made the sketch his own. It would be performed many times long after his death, and in different variations. But *Billy Buttons* was his creation. In this act Astley elevated the role of the horse to a performer in its own right. It was no longer the vehicle solely to display the 'manly feats' of the rider, but became an integral part of the performance. Astley would appear in some form of comic costume, disguised as Billy Buttons, the tailor. The horse would be standing still but when Billy Buttons tried to mount it would walk off, leaving him flat on his face. This would have been repeated several times. Eventually, he managed to mount the horse but found himself facing the wrong way. He had to dismount in order to remount facing the right way. When he did finally mount, the horse lowered its head and promptly deposited him on the ground. Thus the routine continued, each time the horse getting the better of the rider until eventually Billy Buttons chased the horse around the arena, only to end up being chased by the horse. Finally, he managed to mount, threw off his costume to reveal himself as Philip Astley and continued with his exhibitions. It was a very popular routine, and continued to be so throughout the ages, appearing in many versions in many later circuses.

Contrary to popular Astleian mythology, Astley did not immediately fill his venue with jugglers and acrobats and thereby create the 'circus'. This formative move was first made in September 1768 by Astley's rivals, the Woltons who were performing at the nearby Dog and Duck Inn. In association with a Mr. Wilkinson and pupils at a fund-raising show in aid of a burnt-out property in Southwark, their demonstrations of horsemanship were interspersed with tumbling, rope-dancing, and pistol shooting[3]. Astley was soon to copy this idea for his Christmas entertainments by including tumbling and an equestrian monkey.

By the summer of 1769, Astley moved to a more propitious site at the foot of Westminster Bridge. The *Newcastle Courant* of 1 December 1837 gives an account of this acquisition, drawn from an article in a publication entitled *Colburn's New Monthly* in November 1769;

> In the spring of 1769, he took a piece of ground from an old man on Stangate Street, who informerly [sic] kept a preserve for pheasants there, but at that time a timber-yard; he advanced him 200l. [£200] and had the timber, etc, secured to him by way of mortgage: the old man left England and was never heard of again: at the same time, he found a diamond ring worth 60l. [£60] on Westminster Bridge, which was never advertised. He enclosed the timber-yard ... with a high paling and built a wooden house in the situation of the present entrance [on Westminster Bridge Road]; the lower part he made into stables, and the upper a long room for the gentry. The three rows of seats round the ride had a sort of pent-house covering – the centre was entirely open. He then advertised that slight showers would not prevent performances and that proper music was provided. Long Room 2s. [2 shillings]; Riding School 1s., Open at 4, mount at 5.

The incident of the diamond ring has never been proven and may just be part of the Astleian mythology but what is significant in the above piece is that we have a contemporary description of the embryonic beginnings of Astley's Amphitheatre; a dedicated space for 'circus' activities. Kwint (1994:23) goes on to detail how the venue developed.

> Within another year Astley provided 'a Commodious Room apart for Nobility' situated on the side of the ring next to the road, to which admission was two shillings. Lightly constructed of whitewashed boards over a timber frame, it measured forty metres long. Two years later that, its top was converted into a similarly exclusive gallery.

Astley had now given the 'circus' a place of abode and although individual performers came and went, he retained a permanent core company. Having engaged a Mr. and Mrs. Hughes as riding instructors, this allowed Astley the opportunity to travel to

Paris, where he later constructed an amphitheatre. Indeed, from this point onwards, Astley made regular trips to Paris and it became his second home until his death in 1814. His contribution to the development of the circus in France will be discussed in a later chapter. In 1772, Mr. Hughes left Astley's company to establish his own 'British Riding School' near Blackfriars Bridge. Hughes modelled his venture on Astley but it did create a rivalry between the two companies. Both companies presented a mixture of equestrian and other acts. Child prodigies were to the fore, with Astley presenting his five-year-old son John and Hughes countering with his eight-year-old sister, who went by the flamboyant pseudonym of Clementina Sobiewska. Novelty acts were performed, with 'Polandrics' being popular; a combination of acrobatics and perching on chairs and ladders. Astley also presented Mr. Wildman on horseback with his bees, an act later taken on by Mrs. Astley.

At that time, places of entertainment had to be licensed, either by Royal patent for theatrical performances or by magistrates for music and dancing. In June 1737, an Act had been brought before Parliament pertaining to theatrical representations in public. The Act begins;

> An Act to explain and amend so much of an Act, made in the Twelfth Year of the Reign of Queen Anne, intituled [sic] 'An Act for reducing the Laws relating to Rogues, Vagabonds, sturdy Beggars, and Vagrants, into One Act of Parliament; and for the more effectual punishing such Rogues, Vagabonds, sturdy Beggars, and Vagrants, and sending them whither they ought to be sent, as relates to common Players of interludes. (*Journal of the House of Lords, Volume 23*, June 1737. Parliamentary Archives)

Both Astley and Hughes fell afoul of this legislation and, not having the necessary licences, were forced to close their establishments. To avoid prosecution, Hughes travelled across Europe as far as Russia and Astley embarked on a provincial tour of Britain throughout 1773 and 1774, performing in major towns such as Leeds, Dublin, and Edinburgh. In each of these places, performances were either given in the open air or in existing buildings. In Leeds he performed in King Charles' Croft, an expanse of open ground in the town centre. In Dublin in 1774 he erected a covered area for the public. It was reported in the *Saunder's News-Letter* 3 January 1774 that;

Mr. Astley, having been solicited by numbers to put his Riding School on the Inn Quay, on the same footing as that in London ... he gives this public notice that he is building a Shilling gallery ... Admittance Upper Gallery only one British Shilling, commodious covered Boxes two British Shillings each.

But, similar to his Riding School in London, the central arena must have been open to elements because he prefaces his advertising in the *Hibernian Chronicle* 6 June 1774;

This evening (if the weather permits) at the Riding School on the Inn Quay ...

Later in that year in Edinburgh he was still giving open air performances, as indicated here in the *Caledonian Mercury* 30 November 1774 and 7 December 1774;

Mr. Astley will ride in Comely Gardens (if the weather permits) precisely at twelve o'clock.

And

Each day the sun shines and the weather is not too stormy, Mr. Astley will give a grand display of surprising Feats of Activity etc., not to be equalled in Europe.

He also presented indoor entertainments at the New Tumblers Hall and at the Theatre Royal in Edinburgh. But all of these venues whilst 'on the road' were to be a far cry from his home base at the foot of Westminster Bridge.

Hughes was still out of the country at this time. After a court case in which the verdict was given in his favour, Astley was allowed to reopen his Riding School in 1775, 'his exercises in horsemanship not being prohibited by the Act'. His first major construction was to ensure that all of the seating was placed under cover, although the central arena was still fully open to the sky. Further construction work continued in 1778 and 1779, where the arena was also partially enclosed. The venue was renamed *Astley's New Amphitheatre Riding School* and here we see the first use of the word amphitheatre in connection with Astley. By the close of 1780 the roofing was complete and the amphitheatre was fully enclosed, using wood and canvas, thereby now allowing for 'winter entertainments'. An Italian visitor to London went to Astley's and wrote this description;

> The Theatre is of good construction because it is round. The one half serves to contain the two tiers of gradinate [tiered seating] in the form of an Amphitheatre, and the other half is occupied by the stage and by two lateral decorations. The roof seems as if made of sugar ... and this sugar loaf is sustained by a drum-like structure which contains various windows[4].

This is an interesting description, for although the amphitheatre was now fully enclosed, the central dome structure of the roof allowed for natural daylight to play upon the performance area. Astley had not yet conquered the engineering challenge of constructing an entirely open amphitheatre without restricting the view by using vertical roof supports surrounding the arena. Hence his amphitheatre still followed the constructs of the theatres of the period, with the vertical supports surrounding the arena and the boxes and galleries sitting flush to these. Once enclosed, the space allowed for a more diverse range of entertainment, and although equestrianism was still to the fore, music, song, dance, and theatrical interludes known as Burlettas were also popular. More importantly, the enclosed space now allowed for the intimacy of the ring to be established. The audience almost surrounded the central arena. The proximity of the audience to the action made it feel as if it was a part of it and yet it was another world into which it entered, very different from watching performances in the open air. Charles Dickens gives us a flavour of what a visit to Astley's must have been like, albeit some years later.

> Dear, dear, what a place it looked, that Astley's; with all the paint, gilding, and looking-glass; the vague smell of horses suggestive of coming wonders; the curtain that hid such gorgeous mysteries; the clean white sawdust down in the circus ... the clown who ventured on such familiarities with the military man in boots – the lady who jumped over the nine-and-twenty ribbons and came down safe upon the horse's back – everything was delightful, splendid, and surprising! (*The Old Curiosity Shop* 1841)

The interior of Astley's c.1810. One of a number of colour plates reproduced by the Dutch Dairy Bureau in the 1950s for their album The Colourful World of the Circus. *(Author's collection)*

Hughes still being abroad, Astley now had the monopoly on this style of entertainment. However, this was not to last. Hughes returned to England in 1781 and began to collaborate on a grand project with a dramatist and song-writer named Charles Dibdin to create the *Royal Circus, Equestrian and Philharmonic Academy* at St George's Circus, only about half a mile from Astley's. The Royal Circus, as it became popularly known, opened in November 1782, and it is from this name that we derive the term circus as used for this specific genre of entertainment. Whilst Astley favoured wood as the main construction material for his amphitheatre, Hughes and Dibdin used brick and stone and so could quite rightly be said to have constructed the first permanent stone circus building. An eighteenth century engraving of the Royal Circus shows a large double fronted building with a portico, surrounded by railings. Over the portico is a statue of the winged Pegasus. Extending behind the building is the enclosed arena, stables, and store rooms. The central portico area of the building was the main entrance and the two wings served as the Circus Café and a dwelling respectively. Internally, the arena was opulent. A coloured plate in the *Microcosm of London* shows a large horse shoe shaped arena with a large stage at the open end of the horse show.

Internal View of the ROYAL CIRCUS, S.t Georges fields.

Internal view of the Royal Circus. Contemporary engraving late C18th (Public domain image)

The seated audience is accommodated in the pit surrounding the arena and in two upper galleries, with private boxes abutting the stage. There is a third gallery where members of the audience appear to be standing, presumably at a cheaper entry price. The place is decorated in pinks and golds and the dome above the arena is painted with flying cherubs. The structure of the Royal Circus allowed for 'scenes in the circle' but also now provided a large stage for theatrical presentations. Unfortunately for Hughes, the Royal Circus had not been granted the necessary license. Astley, returning from a European tour in 1782 found that he also was subject to a further licensing issue. Both he and Hughes were arrested as the authorities, or to be specific one particular magistrate, attempted to squash the activities of both men. After a short period in the local Bridewell (prison) and a subsequent court hearing, both men were released and the necessary licenses granted[5]. This was a watershed moment in which circus became recognised and accepted as a popular form of entertainment within its own right, certainly with England. I believe that this was the first legal case where circus, as a performance art, was involved. Astley was later involved in a legal dispute in Paris in 1786 with M. Nicolet, a theatre director who had the sole license in Paris to present feats of tumbling on the stage. This was the first case of its kind in Europe. Astley was licensed for equestrian performances only but managed to ingeniously circumvent the license requirements by presenting tumbling on a stage mounted on the backs of several horses.

Both Astley's Amphitheatre and the Royal Circus reopened in 1783 but whereas the Royal Circus began to suffer from poor management, Astley embarked upon several phases of development for his amphitheatre. By 1786 the amphitheatre was completely refurbished and renamed the *Royal Grove*. A retrospective illustration the *The Graphic* newspaper 18 March 1893 gives us an impression of what the interior must have looked like in 1788. Keeping the basic structure of his amphitheatre, the almost circular arena is surrounded by vertical roof supports with two tiers of galleries flush to the side of the arena. A deep stage is set at one end, with two door entrances either side of the proscenium arch. The domed roof still has lantern windows to allow natural light in but also there is a large chandelier hanging from the central boss. The canvas roof is decorated with images of foliage and trees, in a *trompe l'oeil* effect to create a seemingly realistic sylvan setting – hence the name the Royal Grove. The ring fence and balustrades are decorated with swags and embellishments, without any mouldings or protuberances to distract from the action in the arena.

The Royal Grove was eventually renamed the *Royal Saloon* but in August 1794 it was totally destroyed by fire, along with several adjoining houses and a public house. At great expense, Astley had the building reconstructed while he continued his performances at the Lyceum Theatre on the Strand, which, for the time he was there, was known as Astley's New Circus. On February 14 1795, *The Times* announced that Astley's Riding School was nearly completed. Astley's New Amphitheatre of the Arts opened in April 1795 to much acclaim. His ever-changing programmes of entertainment now included comic ballets, pantomimes, pony races, and scenes in the circle. Unfortunately, and common for wooden constructed buildings, the amphitheatre was again destroyed by fire in the September of 1803. John Astley was in charge of the amphitheatre at the time, his father being detained in France as a 'prisoner of war' when Napoleon Bonaparte came to power. Astley senior contrived to escape and made his return to London, where he immediately began overseeing the reconstruction work. The new Amphitheatre was opened on Easter Monday in early April 1804. It now had a stone frontage to Westminster Bridge Road, with an attached wooden portico.

Bells' Weekly Messenger 11 March 1804, gives a description of the exterior.

> Astley has affixed a splendid Mercury, mounted upon an aerial Pegasus, on the southern corner of the New Amphitheatre, which, in addition to the popularity of the building itself, attracts the eye of the gazing crowds, who perhaps never before beheld anything like so dashing a Weather-cock. The beauty, splendour, and particular happiness in point of accommodation in every part of this magnificent edifice, will shortly prove a theme of admiration to every beholder.

The interior was described as such in the *Morning Post* 3 April 1804;

> The boxes are painted pea green, edged with pink, the *tout ensemble* of which is particularly pleasing. The gold triage over the stage had a very grand effect. This is surmounted by the arms of the Union painted in a beautiful manner. In the middle of the Theatre a most superb chandelier is suspended, constructed in a novel manner, the branches of which are elegantly cut, and when it is lighted up exhibits a most dazzling and brilliant appearance.

It was, in all descriptions, a sumptuously decorated building, as can be seen in the illustration from *The Colourful World of the Circus*. Charles Dibdin, son of the Charles Dibdin of Royal Circus fame, wrote a description of the now called Royal Amphitheatre in his 1826 work *History and illustrations of the London theatres*[6];

> The front, which is plain and of brick, stands laterally with the houses in Bridge Road, Lambeth, a short distance from Westminster Bridge, the access to the back part of the premises being in Stangate Street. There is a plain wooden portico, the depth of which corresponds with the width of the pavement, and is lighted by large gas lanterns. This leads to the boxes and the pit; the gallery entrance is lower down the street, and separated from the front by several houses.

> The boxes are approached by a plain staircase, at the head of which is a lobby, which is 11' [feet] 9" [inches] in depth, and about 60' wide, with passages behind the side boxes; at the back of the lobby is a fruit room [refreshment

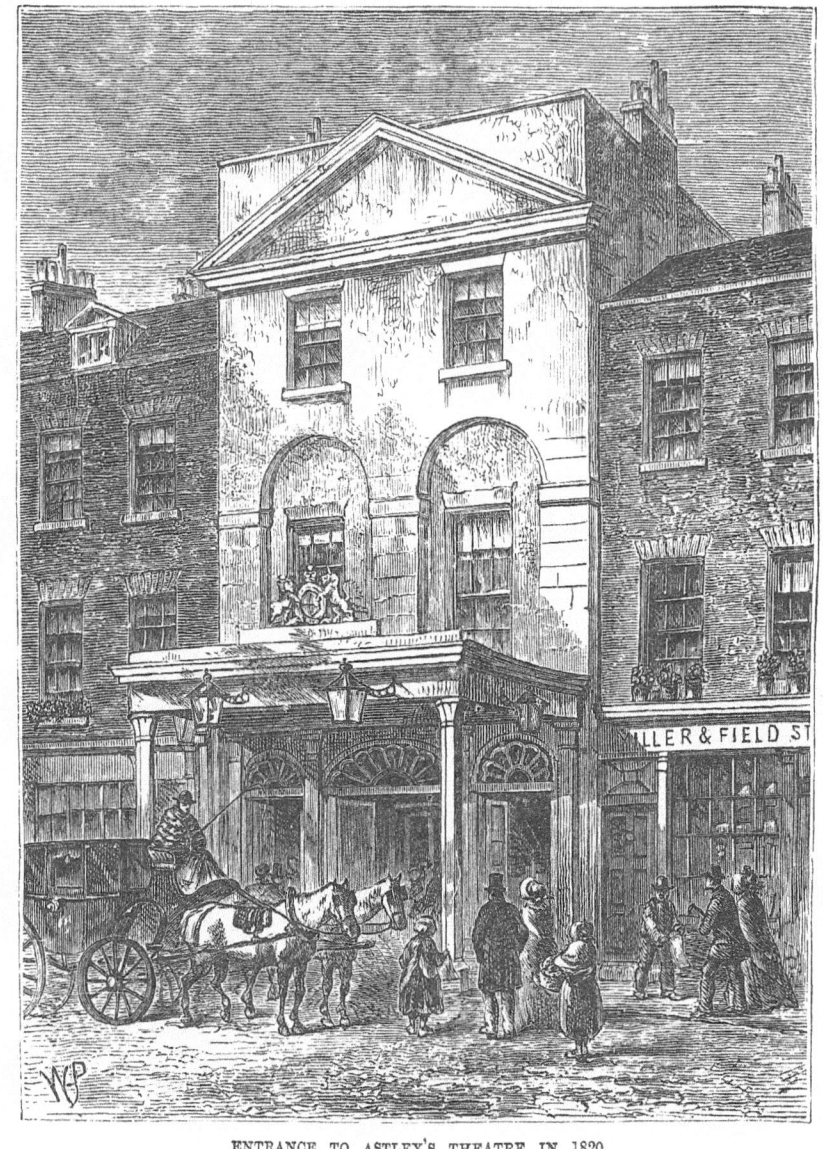

ENTRANCE TO ASTLEY'S THEATRE IN 1820.

Exterior of Astley's Amphitheatre 1820 (Engraving published in Old and New London. *E.Walford 1878)*

room]. There are long seats attached to the wall of the lobby, all round, and in the centre is a large and handsome patent stove. The backs of the boxes, from about 5' from the floor, are entirely open to the lobby, which is customary at most of the minor Theatres. The form of the auditory is elliptical, and is lit by a very large cut lustre, and chandeliers with bell lamps; gas is the medium of illumination used all over the premises.

There is one continual row of tier of boxes around the auditory, above the central part of which is the gallery, and there is a half-tier of upper boxes on each side with slips over them. There are three private boxes on each side adjoining the proscenium, and one at each end of the orchestra. The floor of the ride, within the auditory, is earth and sawdust, where a ring or circle 44' in diameter, is bounded by a boarded inclosure [sic] about 4' in height, the curve of which next the stage forms the outline of the orchestra, and the remainder of the pit behind which is an extensive lobby and bar for refreshments. The proscenium is large and movable, for the convenience of widening and heightening the stage, which is perhaps the largest and most convenient in London, and is terminated by immense platforms or floors, rising above each other and extending the whole width of the stage. These are excessively massive and strong. The horsemen gallop and skirmish over them, and they will admit a carriage equal in size and weight to a mail coach, to be driven across them. They are, notwithstanding, so constructed as to be placed and removed in a short space of time by manual labour and mechanism. When exhibited they are masked with scenery representing battlements, heights, bridges, mountains etc. There are several very considerable inlets and outlets to and from the stage and the stable which communicate.

The stables, which range over a very extensive space of ground on one side of the stage, to the right from the auditory, are very capacious; and when they are wholly occupied by the numbers of beautiful horses attached to the establishment, constitute a most gratifying exhibition. The horses are kept in the most highest [sic] order, and attended by several experienced grooms.

A later piece in the *Illustrated London News* 1 April 1843, when William Batty was the manager, describes Astley's as follows;

The external walls, built by Mr. Buckwell, jnr., of Brighton, are 148 feet in length, and include an area larger than any other theatre in London. There are two fronts; the old one facing Westminster [Bridge] Road ... the other facing the intended new street from Westminster Road to Stangate. This will form the entrance to the gallery. The box-entrance will be, as formerly, from the Westminster Road; thus the two entrances will possess the advantages of being widely separated from each other. The general form of the interior is octagonal ... The prevailing decorations are white, lemon-colour, green and gold, with rich crimson hangings for the private boxes. There are two full tiers of boxes, and two half tiers, ranging evenly from the two galleries. Each of the full tiers contains nineteen open boxes. The circles are supported from the pit by eight Doric pillars and forty-six Corinthian columns, fluted in white and gold. There are six spacious saloons - two for the dress circle, two for the pit, two for the upper boxes, with extensive refreshment places for the galleries. In the centre of the first tier is the royal box, tastefully ornamented ... The decorations consist of copies of the productions of the ancient masters in entablatures of gold. From the rich allegorical dome is suspended a crystal and gold chandelier, emblematic of Fame holding the coursers of triumph ... The stage measures 75 feet by 101, and is fitted with substantial platforms for equestrian spectacles.

Astley's was not the only victim of fire and successive rebuilding. The Royal Circus was destroyed by fire on two occasions. The first was in 1799, after which it was rebuilt in the same style and continued to operate as a circus venue. Suffering a further fire in 1804, it was rebuilt by the famous architect Rudolphe Cabanel. The enterprise was taken over by a manager named Elliston who converted the space into a theatre and the building was renamed the Surrey Theatre in 1809, and performances were now of a dramatic nature. It reverted to presenting circus between 1814 and 1816 but after this date it existed only as a theatre. Astley's remained the pre-eminent circus venue in the capital and continued to do so with several rebuilds and refurbishments until it finally closed its doors in 1893.

By the early part of the nineteenth century, Philip Astley was beginning to take more of a back seat from circus management, leaving it to his son John. But he had one last project in mind, shortly after the New Amphitheatre was rebuilt on Westminster Bridge Road. He leased a piece of land upon which the now demolished Craven House stood, on Wych Street. This was a significant move because it would be his first venture on the north bank of the Thames. The lease was to run for sixty-one years from 29 September 1805, subject to payment of £100 quarterly, clear of all taxes and rates. The terms of the lease were that Astley would agree to erect and furnish a theatre, according to the plans of Lord Craven's surveyor, within four years and to lay out in its completion the sum of £2500. He was also to maintain the building, not to carry out any offensive trade or business on the premises, nor do anything which might cause a nuisance to the neighbouring tenants. The main entrances were on Newcastle Street and Wych Street.

The construction of the *Olympic Pavilion* took over a year to complete. Using timbers from an old French warship, a conoid tent-like structure was erected. The roof was covered with squares of tin sheet which caused strong vibrations to the accompanying music during the performances. The new Olympic Pavilion opened in September 1806, to much acclaim, and within the first week his performances were sold out.

The new venue was considerably smaller than the Amphitheatre and could seat only around 1500 people, as opposed to 2500. This in itself presented a problem but worse was to come in 1810 when the equestrian, Mr. Davis, who had shares in the Amphitheatre, left to set up his own riding school on the Edgeware Road. Attached to the school he erected a Theatre and there presented horsemanship, equestrian feats, and other entertainments, including vaulting, tumbling, tight and slack rope dancing. This was a blow to Astley but, undaunted, he began a programme of enlarging the Pavilion 'to outdo all others'. It was an expensive venture that included strengthening the stage to take the weight of 100 horses. The stage could be altered in shape and enlarged if required. It could also be completely removed for equestrian exercises, but all this took time and was not good for a restless audience. The *Morning Chronicle* of 27 December 1811 described it as;

> A dramatic stage, which takes off like the lid of a snuff box, forming a beautiful scenic bowling-green for the equestrian exercises.

The stage was fifty feet wide, fifty feet high, and sixty feet long, with the scenery and mechanisms required for performances taking up three fifths of the space. To draw the crowds, Astley now introduced pony races. These proved popular and along with the expansive melodramatic spectaculars still attracted an audience. Bigger and better seems to have been the mantra of the Astleys. In January 1812, Astley junior arranged;

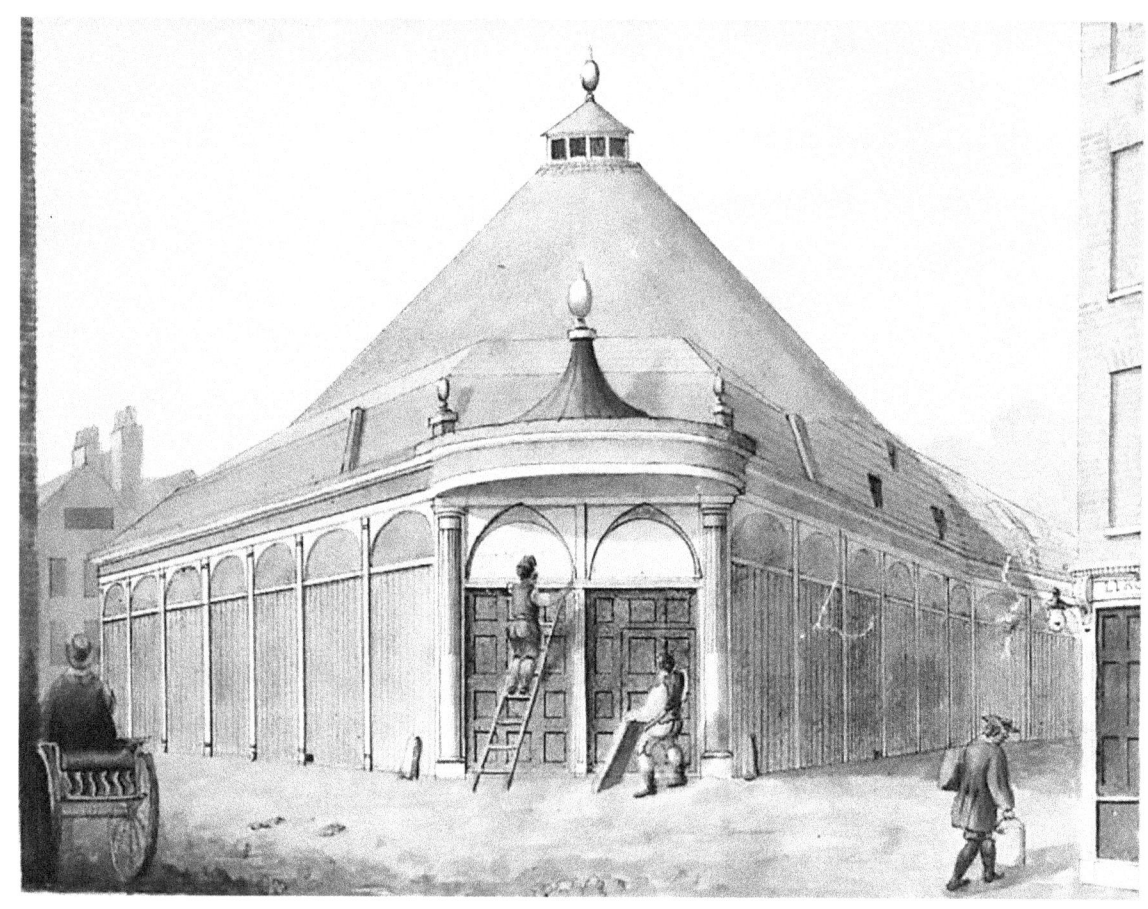

Astley's Olympic Pavilion c. 1806 (Public domain image)

In the course of the Spectacle various splendid processions, introducing the largest and most sagacious Elephant, in this kingdom. (*Morning Chronicle* 21 January 1812)

The elephant belonged to the menagerie owner Mr. Polito and had been procured by Astley at tremendous expense, probably the first elephant to be used in public performance; as opposed to being on display in a menagerie. But after this highlight of the winter season, the entertainments at the Olympic Pavilion the following season were reduced to comic songs, dances, pantomimes and harlequinades. The grand spectacles were too elaborate and expensive to stage, and the box office takings did not warrant the outlay. The Westminster Bridge Amphitheatre was still going from strength to strength, with seemingly more expansive hippodramatic spectacles. Astley senior was reduced to including pugilistic sparring (boxing) contests as entertainments. Audience numbers dwindled and the days of the Pavilion were numbered. He decided to put the Pavilion on the market and soon Robert Elliston, formerly at the Surrey Theatre, made him an offer of 3000 guineas and an annuity of £100 per annum. Astley readily accepted and retired to Paris, where he died in 1814.

By the time of his death there were amphitheatres built in many of the larger towns and cities across the United Kingdom and Europe. Some were permanent in the sense that they provided a continuous site for circus activities, even if the actual buildings, chiefly of wood, were subsequently rebuilt and refurbished. Others were permanent in the sense that they were constructed of stone or brick. Whichever they were, there is no doubt that Astley's buildings became the model for circus venues for many years to follow.

Notes

1. Diary entries from September 1668 (The Diary of Samuel Pepys). Online at; pepysdiary.com)

2. From *A Retrospective of the Dublin Stage* online at; https://www.libraryireland.com

3. The *Gazetteer* 10 September 1768. British Library *Lyson's Collecteana* vol 4 f21

4. Published Edward Gordon Craig in *The Mask* 1929

5. A fuller account of this is given in; Ward. S, (2018) *Father of the Modern Circus; Billy Buttons; The Life & Times of Philip Astley.* Pen & Sword.

6. Published Moyes. London, 1826

CHAPTER 2

THE ASTLEY LEGACY

By the time that Philip Astley died in 1814, circus was becoming well established. As well as the Royal Circus and Astley's Amphitheatre in London, other circuses are recorded across Britain. A trawl through the British Library newspaper archives for 1814 saw circuses in Exeter and Bristol in the west, Limerick and Dublin in Ireland, Edinburgh in Scotland, and other major towns such as Liverpool, Leeds, York, Hull, Manchester, and Chester. There were now other circus owners who had equestrian troupes on tour; Bannister, Matthews, Charlatan, West, Moritz, Wild, Kemp, Davis, Bridges, Cummings, and Peters. Most of these performances would have been given in rapidly erected temporary wooden structures; construction material was plentiful and labour was cheap. Some of these buildings would have been used for a short time only before being taken down and the materials auctioned off. On other sites, the buildings would have been refurbished, or in some cases rebuilt, as new circuses arrived. In fact, in central Leeds one particular circus site on Boar Lane was in use for almost sixty years; the first being erected in 1805 and the last recorded use in 1862. The wooden amphitheatre was the standard design for circuses for many years to come. These buildings may have been designed as temporary wooden structures but that is not to say that they were not well appointed. When Cooke's Circus visited Leeds in 1839 the exterior of the building was referred to in a news report as 'resembling in external appearance a Roman Temple'. The same report goes on to describe the interior;

> The interior of the Circus will present a style of Elegant Decorations perfectly novel, and combining the extremes of classical neatness, and every variety of magnificent ornament. The Boxes embellished in a superior manner, with every attention to comfort and convenience. The Pit will be found spacious, and will command a distinct and full view of every part of the Circle. The Gallery has every accommodation to render the visitors comfortable. The Decorations over the ring will be superb, including a splendid Ceiling, suspended from which will be a massive candelabra, emitting hundreds of

illuminated Jets [gaslights]; mounted Banners of the various nations of the world, and grand Equestrian Emblems. (*Leeds Times* 6 July 1838)

The following year, Cooke took his circus to Wakefield where a wooden circus was built on Wood Street. Following his performances there the circus building was taken down and another building constructed there a few years later;

> A new circus has just been erected in Wood Street, by Messrs. Depledge and Speight, builders, of this town, for Wallet and Woodward's company of equestrians, who are about to pay this town a visit. It is 84 feet long by 48 feet wide, and the ring is 126 feet in circumference. It is a firm, substantial wood building, replete with boxes, pit, and gallery. Its erection has cost £120 [This sum would be an equivalent of just over £7000 today]. (*Leeds Times* 21 May 1842)

There are some interesting points from the above reports. The first is that these buildings were substantial and internally well-appointed. It is clear that a gas supply was installed in the Leeds amphitheatre. The second point is that, although we may think of circus buildings as being round, in fact they were often rectilinear, as in the case of the Wakefield building. The ring, and in the Wakefield building it was just over forty feet in diameter, was contained within what otherwise was a quadrangular building. Paul Bouissac makes mention of this in his 2022 conference paper *The Otherness of Circus Space*[1];

> ... the nineteenth century in Europe witnessed the building of stone, steel, and wood circuses in the centre of major cities. Many of these buildings have preserved the circularity in their outside architecture ... But some buildings have complied with the quadrangular norms of their urban setting by appearing as straight façades that blend with the surrounding architecture ...

It is worth noting that across continental Europe many circus buildings were indeed either round or elliptical but in Britain, the home of the modern circus, buildings temporary and permanent were predominantly rectilinear.

Wooden structures were prone to all sorts of calamities. Fire was the most common. Both the Royal Circus and Astley's were destroyed on two occasions each; the Royal Circus in 1799 and 1804, and Astley's in 1794 and 1803. A contemporary account paints a horrific picture of the destruction of Astley's for the second time;

FIRE AT ASTLEY'S AMPHITHEATRE

On Friday morning, between two and three o'clock, this beautiful and superb edifice situated on the Surrey side of Westminster bridge, was discovered to be on fire. The flames, which must have been long collected in the interior burst from the roof off the building like a volcano, illuminating for a while the whole horizon, and threatening with destruction a considerable part of the very crowded and populous neighbourhood. How or in what part of the Theatre this calamity began has not yet been ascertained. It is the second visitation of this kind which has befallen the always loyal and patriotic but now unfortunate Astleys – the old gentleman is at present captive in France; an affectionate wife, a prey to death in his absence, but two days buried; and now the whole of his property, and with it the means of his family's subsistence, a sacrifice to an all devouring conflagration, which, raging with uncontroulable [sic] fury for upwards of three hours has desolated not less than eleven houses in the rear of the Amphitheatre. These were inhabited by persons in ordinary circumstances who, shivering and naked in the streets, were glad to escape with their lives. To add to the calamity, Mrs. Woodman, mother-in- law to young Mr. Astley, perished in the flames. She was far advanced in life, but was seen running from window to window, imploring that help which two neighbours, Mr. Burton and Mr. Moor, were hastening with a ladder to afford her, when the floor fell in and put a period, forever, to her sufferings. Her headless trunk has since been dug out of the ruins. Two children belonging to a poor man who inhabited one of the houses that has been destroyed, had nearly perished, but were most providentially saved. (*The Aberdeen Journal* 7 September 1803)

But, being made of wood they were quickly able to be rebuilt. However, accidents also happened during construction. In March 1871, a wooden circus building was being erected in Bolton for the circus of Charles Adams. The circus was given as being 100 feet in length, 60 feet in width and 34 feet high. The architect was Edward Harrison and it is clear from the inquest into the collapse of the roof under construction, and death of two workers, that he was well accustomed to building wooden circuses both in Britain and across the Continent. The lengthy inquest report, and a later illustration in the *Illustrated Police News* of 11 March 1871, also gives us an idea of the general construction of such buildings;

Bolton circus collapse. Illustrated Police News *11 March 1871 (Author's collection)*

He [witness] was employed ... to assist in building the circus, and was at the very top of the roof at the time of the accident. At that time the derrick was standing up at the end ... inside the building. It was the north end of the building. There was a guy rope at the opposite end, attached to one of the principals at the top of the building ... the other end being attached to an iron bar in the ground ... Heard Mr. Edward Thomas Harrison, the architect, give directions to John Rigby, the joiner, to loosen the rope, as he said it was doing no good. John Rigby and Mr. Harrison then pulled it up. They did not pull the iron to which one end of the rope was fixed out of the stones. They untied the rope at the top of the roof – that was the rope which was attached to the principal. The result of that proceeding was that in about a quarter of an hour or twenty minutes afterwards the roof fell in.

Harrison then gave his evidence;

> ... said he was employed by Mr. Adams in the erection of his circuses generally. He had been so engaged on the Continent as well. He had been in the habit of building four circuses in the year for over 30 years but the present accident was the first that ever occurred with him ... Mr. Harrison further said there were persons present who stated that the wind had caused the fall ... He had frequently removed the guy rope from the principal to the collar beam, and the rope in question was removed in order to better enable the men to fix in the boards.

At first sight it might seem that Harrison was responsible for the accident but the coroner went on to instruct the jury;

> It did not appear to him that any person having charge of the building could be held liable to a criminal prosecution, ordinary care and discretion having been used by those in charge of the work, and no person could be held criminally responsible for the accident. Mr. Harrison had exercised his usual judgement, and erected that building as he had on upwards of 100 previous occasions.

The jury then retired and returned the following verdict;

> That the deceased came by their deaths accidentally, and the jury attributed the cause of the roof giving way to an indiscretion of the architect ordering the removal of the guy rope from the south end. (*Bolton Evening News* 7 March 1871)

Apart from Harrison having been found guilty of an 'indiscretion' there is no record of him receiving any sanction, neither is there any record of the deceased's dependents or those injured receiving any compensation.

I think there are some points that we can gather from this report. The circus building went on to be completed after the accident, so the two fatalities did not deter the workmen and the damage was readily repaired; labour was cheap and materials plentiful. If Harrison had been building wooden circuses for over thirty years at a rate of four per year, and assuming that he was not the only architect doing so, then even in 1871 the wooden circus building appears to have been the norm.

If wooden circuses were successfully completed there was always the danger that they could collapse. This famously happened in Leeds in 1848. During an evening performance of Pablo Fanque's circus;

SHOCKING ACCIDENT
AT MR. PABLO FANQUE'S CIRCUS
DEATH OF MRS. FANQUE AND NARROW
ESCAPE OF MANY OTHER PERSONS

A serious and fatal accident occurred at the Circus – a temporary wooden erection – occupied by Mr. W. Darby, better known by the name of Pablo Fanque, and his corps of equestrians in Kings Charles' Croft Leeds, at about a quarter to ten o'clock on Saturday night last. The performances were for the benefit of Mr. Wallett, the celebrated comic jester or clown, and the circus was crowded in every part, many persons having had to be refused admission owing to the want of room. All went on well, till the hour above named, at which time Pablo Fanque Junior was performing some feats on the tight rope, when suddenly that portion called the pit, which was a kind of wooden chamber, built in a sloping position upon a framework of wood, fell to the ground with a tremendous crash. There were upwards of six hundred persons, of all ages and both sexes, in the pit at the time and the most of these fell with the broken and loosened timber and planks of which it was composed; some of them fell into the gallery which adjoined the front of the pit, but was on a lower level; and many fell into the lobby of the building, and others out at one side; the weight of the falling timber and the people together bursting out a portion of that side of the circus the nearest to Land's Lane. Mrs. Darby and Mrs. Wallett were both in the lobby at the time of the melancholy occurrence. They were both thrown down and, we regret to say, that two heavy planks fell upon the back part of the head and neck of Mrs. Darby and killed her on the spot. Mrs. Wallett received some severe bruises and contusions but she is fast recovering. Many other persons were injured but none, we believe, seriously. The gas with which the circus was lighted was put out by some of the pipes being broken in the fall and the scene presented immediately after the erection had given way was one of indescribable alarm and confusion. (*The Leeds Mercury* 25 March 1848)

There was of course a lot of speculation as to what had happened to cause the accident and fingers were pointed in several directions. Pablo Fanque explained that he had taken the circus on, having heard it was safe and having had it examined by his own architect. The joiner who had built the circus then stated that he had built it for a previous circus owner, Charles Hengler, under the direction of his architect. He was rather vague as to how the gallery had been propped but he suggested that some of Hengler's men may have removed some of the props when they removed their equipment from the circus. He had let the building to Fanque 'as it stood' and he was to make any alterations that he required 'at his own expense'. Who was responsible for this calamity? The coroner could not find any culpable negligence and declared that the accident had arisen, in all probability, from some error of judgement and that the death of Mrs. Susannah Darby, the wife of Pablo Fanque, was 'accidental'.

As with the previous report, there are some interesting snippets of information. The circus building was referred to as 'temporary', even though the building had been previously used by another company. There is a good description of the layout of the interior, which was typical of such buildings. Also worth noting is that a gas supply had been installed in the building by this date. If such buildings were considered temporary then it seems a lot of work to have a gas supply piped in if it was only being used for such a relatively short time. The Bolton circus, mentioned above, was estimated to have been constructed within a month; a significant amount of effort for a temporary building. I think that they were more semi-permanent rather than temporary. They would have been used for several seasons, by different companies; each company refurbishing the building as necessary.

Given that fires and collapses were not uncommon it is surprising that more permanent brick-built circuses were not more widely constructed. It is true that some circuses did perform in adapted theatres and music halls while on tour during the nineteenth century. In these cases, the seating was removed from what we now term the 'stalls' and a circus ring constructed in the space. Sketches of both interiors of the Royal Circus and Astley's Amphitheatre show a similar lay out and this does seem to be the standard for circus design during this period, irrespective of whether in a wooden or stone-built circus.

It was mentioned in the last chapter that the Royal Circus was the first purpose-built circus building in stone. Astley's Amphitheatre later became clad in stone, although still having a wooden interior construction. It is often said that Astley created the first stone-built amphitheatre in Dublin when he first went there in 1773/4. This is not accurate, as his first performances were given at the Inns Quay on the banks of the river Liffey[2]. There is a contemporary illustration used on the Circopedia website[3] entitled *Astley's Amphitheatre in Dublin (circa 1790)*.

Molyneux House 1790. The site of the Dublin Amphitheatre (Public domain image)

This image regularly appears on various websites and shows a large stone-built house, from the flagpole of which is a banner announcing *Amphitheatre*. This is taken as evidence that the building shown was actually the amphitheatre itself. This is not so. Philip Astley leased the premises, known as Molyneux House, on Peter Street from the Molyneux family. Here, he and his family resided when they were in Dublin. The actual amphitheatre was an extension to the rear of the building and was constructed of wood and canvas, evidenced as follows. *A House of Commons Report upon the Principal*

Charitable Institutions of Dublin, dated May 1, 1835, contains a favourable account of the Molyneux Asylum, the account beginning as follows:

> Until the year 1815 there did not exist any institution whatever in Ireland for the support, relief, or education of the female poor who were afflicted by the loss of sight. In the early part of that year, or latter part of the preceding year, the Rev. John Crosthwaite communicated to Mr. Hughes and Mr. Ferrier the design of such an institution; a house was accordingly taken and a prospectus issued, and on 1st June 1815 the institution was opened, though at that time the funds were not sufficient for its support. Astley's Amphitheatre (which formed part of the premises taken by the trustees) a building which consisted of upright posts, supporting a canvass covering, was converted, by substituting walls for the posts, into a chapel for the celebration of divine services, according to the forms of the Church of England, to which a roof was added after the expiration of about six years.[4]

The move towards more permanent stone-built circus structures was not as fast as some people would make out. Wooden and canvas structures were still favoured by touring companies, especially if they were to be in one location for any length of time. Other companies operated in large canvas marquees or 'pavilions' as they were often billed. These were not yet of the circular kind that we associate with the American 'Big-Top' but tended to be of a rectangular construction, with the ring and associated seating erected inside. Apart from the Royal Circus in London, one of the first purpose built stone circuses in Britain was created by Frederick Charles Hengler in Liverpool in 1857.

'Charles' Hengler was born in Cambridge, England, in 1820. He came from a long line of circus performers. His grandfather Michael Hengler was a German equestrian and pyrotechnic expert who first arrived in England around 1780 and established Hengler's Firework Company. Astley was among his customers. His father, Henry, one of ten children to Michael, was a renowned tight-rope dancer who worked with Andrew Ducrow for many years, during which time he introduced his three sons to the business; altogether he had twelve children. Henry Hengler then went on to work with Price and Powell's circus and it was here that Charles began his involvement with the circus business, moving from being a theatrical musician to working in the business department of Price and Powell. The circus was eventually sold to Charles and his brother Edward, and when Edward retired around 1851, Charles became the sole proprietor. Although having been involved with touring he made his base of operations in Liverpool and it is here that he must have seen the opportunity to erect his first purpose-built circus building. He became a prolific builder of permanent circus buildings and over a period of almost fifty years, he built three successive circuses within the city and several others around the country. His son Albert Hengler continued the business after his father died in 1887.

His first venture, aptly named Hengler's Cirque, was built on the site of a well-known inn on Dale Street called the Saracens' Head, which was demolished in 1855. It opened in March 1857 and existed until 1861. McMillan (2018:84) informs us that;

> The circus was within a brick and stone wall with a majestic arched entrance-
> way. It was a circular wooden building with a conical roof and a ventilation
> on top.

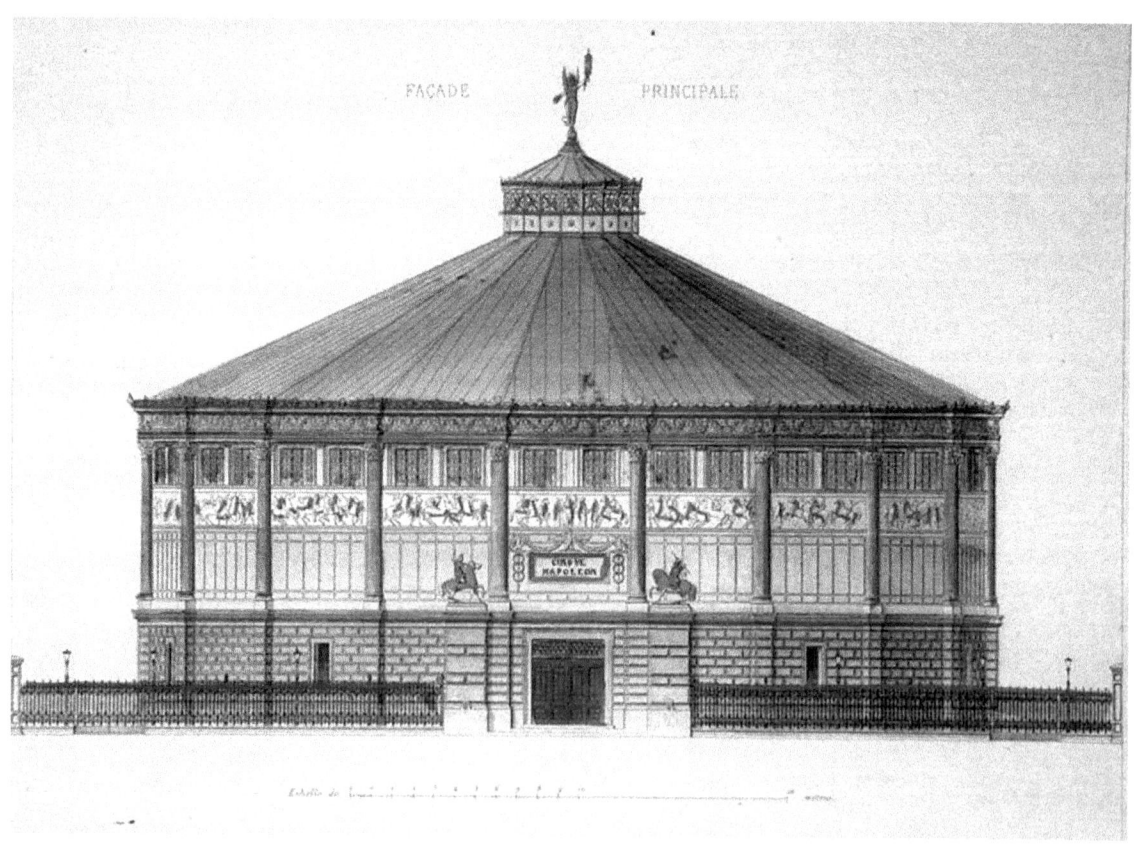

Cirque Napoleon facia design. Hittorf J. 1852 (Public domain image)

Although permanent in the sense that it was used for four successive years, it was still essentially a wooden construction. It was constructed in the style of the Cirque Napoleon in Paris, France, which had been built in 1852. The Cirque Napoleon is claimed to be the oldest circus building in the world, although the Royal Circus in London opened some seventy years earlier. However, the Cirque Napoleon building became the Cirque National, and then later the Cirque d'Hiver.

So, in terms of continuity of use the claim has some justification, as we shall see in a later chapter. A notice of the opening of Hengler's Cirque announced that;

> (it) will be found replete in every possible arrangement for the comfort of the vast audience ... The first- and second-class boxes are carpeted throughout, and furnished with cushioned seats. The spacious Promenade, 200 feet (61 metres) in length, encircles three quarters of the building, from every part of which an uninterrupted view of the arena is commanded. A magnificent canopy will cover the interior of the building, which will be interspersed with flags of all nations and emblem designs, red, white, and blue being the characteristics of the decoration. The whole brilliantly illuminated with gas ... Compartments for visitors are partitioned off, with a separate and convenient approach to each. Reserved Seats or Stalls (select) 3s, Half Price 1s 6d; Boxes (select) 2s, Half Price 1s 0d; Second Seats 1s, Half Price 0s 6d; Gallery 6d, No Half Price; Promenade 1s, No Half Price ... Order and decorum will be strictly enforced. Police-officers will be in attendance. (*Liverpool Mail*, 7 March 1857)

It is interesting to note that Hengler wished to reassure his public that the peace would be kept by attending police officers. Circuses of the period were frequently disrupted by disturbances, as here in the *South Wales Daily Telegram* of 17 August 1874;

> During the present week Messrs. Sanger's circus has been exhibiting in Parliament Fields ... near the suburbs of Manchester and has drawn together large crowds of roughs. On Thursday, a mob of some thousands broke into the show, and after severe struggling with some thirty of forty men employed by Messrs. Sanger and a dozen police, in which sticks, stones, and

other weapons were used, the equestrian members of the troupe charged the mob and expelled them. One jockey was so injured that he was removed to the hospital, and altogether twenty or thirty persons were injured. After expulsion the roughs had a free fight amongst themselves for about an hour.

The land upon which Hengler's Cirque had been built was bought by the Liverpool Hotel Company in 1861, and the final performance at this venue was given on March 14 1861. This was announced in the *Liverpool Mail* of 9 March 1861;

> Mr. C. Hengler respectfully and cordially returns thanks to the Nobility, Gentry, and the Inhabitants of Liverpool ... and begs to inform them that Thursday Evening, March 14th, is positively the last performance that can take place in the present building, as it will be taken down to make room for the erection of the new Liverpool Hotel; but should it be his fortune to obtain another site on which again to erect a Cirque, he assures them that no pains or expense shall be spared to produce a Building and Performance in every way worthy of this great town.

And this is exactly what he did. Hengler went on to construct his New Grand Cirque Variété in Cropper Street in the October of that same year, the architects being Holme and Nicol. He continued in this venue until the close of the 1870 winter season, after which time the building was later demolished.

Although Hengler spent time in several towns and cities around the country during the 1860s, he went on to build a third circus in Liverpool, Hengler's Grand Cirque in West Derby Road, opening in 1876.

The front elevation was constructed of red pressed bricks with ornamental drawings of classical design. In the front of the building were five shops, with the principal entrance to the Cirque in the centre, behind iron ornamental gates. This central entrance led to the stalls and boxes. A contemporary article[5] stated that the seating was arranged to give a clear view of the arena. There were five private boxes, 200 reserved stalls, 600 seats in the parterre, 2000 in the Pit and Balconies, and 1600 in the Galleries – a total of spaces for 4500 people. The front and side balconies had ornamental fronts, the caps of pillars having the Prince of Wales's feathers. In the spandrels of the arches were

*Hengler's Cirque on West Derby Road, Liverpool (*The Builder *1876)*

large trophies and flags of all nations. The decorations were carried out in gold on a mauve and pink ground. An extra ring fence was fitted to prevent the soil being kicked into the faces of the audience. At the rear of the building there was stabling for fifty horses and a carriage shed along with adequate dressing rooms and wardrobes. It was also pointed out that the construction of the roof was novel in design, the span being one hundred feet, and the collar beam was eighteen feet from the feet of the double principal rafters; one and a half inch tension rods were placed from the feet between these rafters, running to the bottom of the king-post (the king post being the central vertical post from the cross beam to the apex of the roof triangle), and thence to the top of the same, thus forming a light timbered roof and an iron one at the same time; nine inch by three inch Purlins were placed every three feet, resting on the principals and were covered over with dry one and a half inch boards, and then slated. A syphon ventilator was formed in the centre of the roof, twelve feet square, and inlets of cold air were fixed in convenient places to assist ventilation and avoid draughts. The ceiling was constructed of wood and canvas, formed into panels and ribs, with bosses (a key stone of wood, metal or stone used in roof vaulting) at each intersection of the ribs, from which dropped twelve brass chandeliers, each containing fifty gas lights. The sunlight had a domed silver-plated reflector over it, which was apparently the idea of Hengler himself.

What is notable about the plans for this building is that the stage that was so evident in the earlier circus buildings, such as the Royal Circus and Astley's Amphitheatre, has now been dispensed with.

Hengler's circus building now contains the ring as the central feature, with seating surrounding it, and with two separate ring entrances. This now begins to separate the circus as a distinct art form from the theatre. Circus is a visceral art form; it is a spectacle of actuality (Coxe, 1951:17-18). Circus performers present their skills in real time; they do not *pretend* to perform their skills, they *do* them. Theatre is the art of artifice; it is a representation of reality, not reality itself. As soon as the stage was removed from circus building design, the focus of the performed activity became the central ring – an iconic image in modern circus. However, some later constructed circus buildings did retain a stage for light dramatic interludes or for acts that could not be presented within a ring. An example of this would be the 1853 'ceiling walking' act of Richard Sands, the American circus owner. With rubber suction pads attached to his feet, he would walk upside down across a suspended wooden ceiling. Tragedy befell him in 1861 when

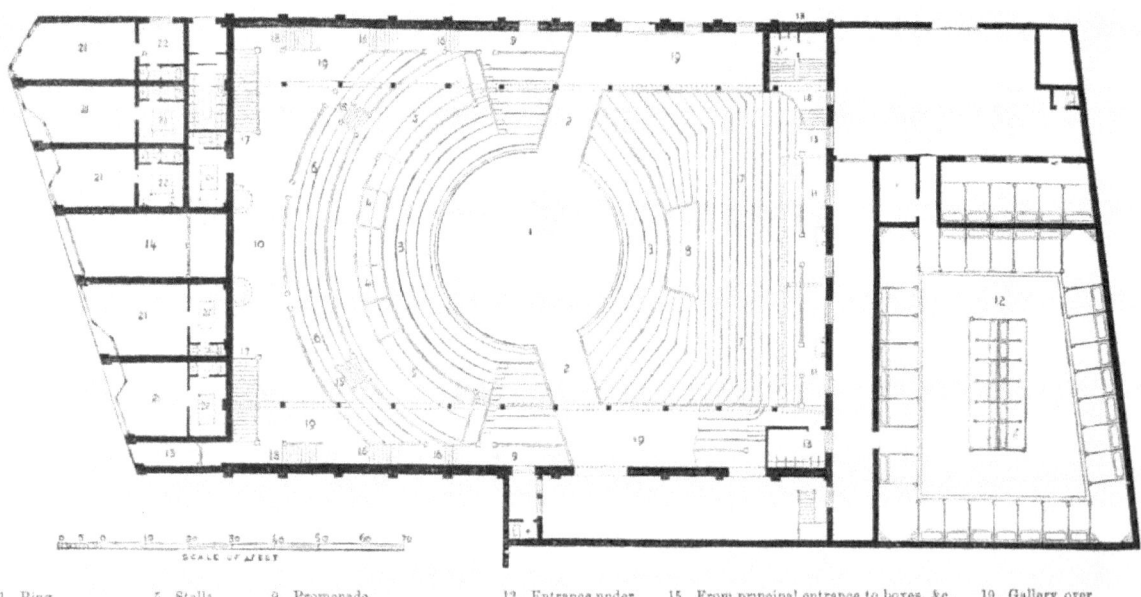

1. Ring.	5. Stalls.	9. Promenade.	13. Entrance under.	15. From principal entrance to boxes, &c.	19. Gallery over.
2. Entrance to ring.	6. Pit.	10. Promenade : gallery over ; pay-boxes under.		16. Steps down.	20. Ladies' cloak-room.
3. Parterre.	7. Gallery.	11. Promenade : property-rooms under.		17. Steps up.	21. Shops.
4. Boxes.	8. Orchestra.	12. Stables.	14. Principal entrance under.	18. Gallery-stairs.	22. Sitting-rooms.

HENGLER'S NEW CIRQUE, WEST DERBY ROAD, LIVERPOOL.——Mr. J. T. Robinson, Architect.

Floor plan of Hengler's Cirque (The Builder *1876*)

performing in Melrose, Massachusetts. A section of plaster to which he was attached gave way and he fell to his death. It is also worth noting that Hengler's Grand Cirque conforms to the rectilinear plan so favoured by British circuses, as opposed to the contemporary Parisian counterpart of the Cirque Napoleon which was circular in design.

Hengler's Cirque as the Liverpool Hippodrome. Early C20th postcard (Author's collection)

On opening night, 13th November 1876, Hengler was quick to announce in detail those who had contributed to the construction and decoration of the building;

THIS NEW AND MAGNIFICENT CIRQUE, the largest and most complete ever erected within the United Kingdom, and occupying an area of 20,000 square feet [1850 square metres or about three times the playing area of a standard soccer pitch], elegantly decorated and luxuriously upholstered WILL OPEN TONIGHT ... The following business firms have been engaged in the construction of the building and the supply of its interior fittings, viz; Architect, Mr. J. T. Robinson, Surveyor of Theatres to the Lord Chamberlain. Contractor, Mr. Samuel Campbell, of Liverpool. The ceiling and general decorations have been carried out under the superintendence of Mr. Thomas Rogers, scenic artist, of London. The ornamental panels and other devices in *carton pierre* [a paper-pulp mix used to imitate stone or bronze and used for architectural ornamentation] are the work of George Jackson and Sons, of London; while Mr. Rohrer and Saul Moss and Co., of Liverpool, have also contributed to the gilding and painting. The upholstering is by Villars and Son, London; Ray and Miles, Liverpool; and Audas and Leggott, of Hull. The chandeliers are from R. W. Winfield and Co., Birmingham; and the gas fittings from Mr. Price, of Church Street, Liverpool, and Z. D. Berry and Son, of London. Mr. R. W. Smith, of Williamson Square, has supplied the carpets; and the electric bells throughout the building have been placed by Mr. Butler; the whole having been carried out under the personal supervision of MR. CHARLES HENGLER. (*Liverpool Mercury* 13 November 1876)

Clearly, Hengler's Grand Cirque was a mammoth undertaking and drew upon craftsmen from all over the country. It was a far cry from the relatively hastily erected wooden buildings still in common use. Hengler's Grand Cirque ran as a successful circus venue for almost twenty-five years. Unfortunately, Charles Hengler died in 1887 and it was his son Albert Hengler who continued as manager until it closed in February 1901. The building remained unoccupied for a short while and was then bought and redeveloped into a Variety Theatre. The interior was gutted but the exterior shell kept intact. It opened in August 1902 as the Liverpool Hippodrome and existed until 1931, when it became a cinema. This closed in 1970 and the building finally demolished in 1980.

We should now explore Hengler's contribution to the establishment of his circus building empire throughout the United Kingdom.

Notes

1. Bouissac, P. (January 2022) The Otherness of Circus Space; When the circus entered history. *International academic conference address Budapest; Circus Buildings in Europe.* Unpublished address transcript.

2. *Saunder's News-letter* 5 January 1774

3. http://www.circopedia.org/Astley%27s_Amphitheatre

4. Molyneux House - Upper Leeson Street Area Dublin Walking Tour - PocketSights

5. *The Builder* – An illustrated Weekly Magazine. Vol. 34 p1168. 2 December 1876

CHAPTER 3

THE HENGLER EMPIRE

In terms of establishing circuses throughout the country it is fair to say that Hengler was the greatest circus impresario of the age. Although some of his later buildings are more well known, especially that of the Grand Cirque in Liverpool, some of his earlier buildings are also worthy of note. He made his first visit to Ireland in 1860, setting up a large circus building in Dublin on land adjoining the Westland Row railway station. This was an important and relatively judicious choice of site as it allowed visitors from outside of the city to easily attend the circus. Hengler's Grand Cirque opened on Easter Monday and the *Dublin Evening Mail* of 28 March gave this advertisement;

The most complete Cirque ever erected in Great Britain or Ireland, constructed by experienced builders and architect, decorated in magnificent style, brilliantly illuminated with gas. SPLENDID BANDS and a Troupe of Artistes unrivalled in their different departments ... Mr. C. H. would respectfully impress upon the mind of the public that his is the only Cirque (proper) that has ever been erected in Dublin. The circumference of the main building is 300 feet; the interior divided into compartments for Stalls, Boxes, Second Class Promenade, and Gallery. The Stalls and Boxes are carpeted throughout, and velvet cushioned chairs placed to afford each visitor ample space; the Second-Class Seats covered, with ample room for each; the Gallery set apart; and a Promenade of 200 feet, being elevated behind the Stalls and Boxes, will be found a delightful Lounge; the whole interior covered with a magnificent Canopy, ornamented and painted emblematic of the Emerald Isle [a popular term for Ireland]. From the centre hangs a massive gasalier of 120 lights, and eight smaller ones. The whole of the ring for the performance is covered with carpet and cocoa-nut fibre matting, so that from the rapid evolution of the horse not the least dust arises ... Order and decorum rigidly enforced and any visitor giving offence to the audience will be instantly expelled. Smoking strictly prohibited.

A later report in the same publication on 11 April, after the Cirque had opened for the season, adds to the description of the interior;

> Its interior presented a most brilliant aspect. The eight fine statues, nearly life-size, which are made to represent Caryotides [sic; a carving of a draped female figure used as a pillar in Greek style buildings], on the front section of uprights supporting the roof, looked exceedingly graceful, being thrown out into bold relief by the mellow light diffused through the building from a splendid series of chandeliers, and from the jets which encircled the cornice of the amphitheatre. The white and crimson draperies which covered the ceiling threw a rich, warm tone over the interior, and had a singularly grand effect. The centre of the circus arena is richly carpeted, and the radius section set apart for the performance of the horses. The carpeted section is thus adapted for acrobatic feats, and for the exquisitely comic tricks of the rival clowns ... and owing to the perfect character of the ventilation, we were gratified to perceive that the stable odour, so irrepressibly and disagreeably prominent in most equestrian theatres, was altogether absent.

This clearly was a sumptuously and well-appointed construction, with special thought given to the ventilation system. The implication of the first description is that the building was of circular construction, having a diameter of just over 95 feet. The second description refers to it as an amphitheatre, a commonly used term for timber-built circuses of the time. Although some may claim that this was Dublin's first permanent circus building, it was likely to have been constructed largely of wood and canvas. A later news report referred to it as a 'spacious and splendid pavilion', the term pavilion supporting this line of thought. Hengler remained in Dublin until the end of July 1860, after which time he moved his company to Belfast. Interestingly, an advertisement column for Hengler's Grand Cirque Varieté in the *Banner of Ulster* newspaper of 4 August, to open in Belfast on 8 August, carried an almost identically worded description of his circus to that which appeared in the *Dublin Evening Mail* on 28 March. It is clear that these Grand Cirques were intended as semi-permanent structures to be used for a season in one location, before moving on to the next one. There is no evidence to suggest that the Cirque in Dublin was dismantled and the materials auctioned off, as with some wooden amphitheatres, so it is possible that much of the building was designed as being transportable. Sadly, they were also prone to fires. In 1864, it was reported that;

> Hengler's Circus, a large establishment, just constructed at Belfast, was burnt down on Wednesday morning. One of the horses was burnt to death, and a valuable stock of dresses was also destroyed. The building, just completed, had been given up by the builder to the owner, and was to have been opened at the end of the week. (*Birmingham Journal* 7 May 1864)

Charles Hengler did not return to Dublin until 1869, when he set up his Cirque in the Rotunda Gardens. His season ran from March to July, and again his Cirque was a semi-permanent structure before being dismantled and moving on. McMillan (2018:154) also cites that the circus in the Rotunda Gardens was a wooden construction. The Hengler dynasty developed a long tradition of appearing in the Rotunda Gardens, and Albert Hengler, son of Charles, continued to perform there in the 1880s and 1890s.

Conversions or adaptions of existing buildings were also a common practice for Hengler; why go to the trouble of building a circus from scratch when an existing building could be utilised? In Edinburgh he set up a circus within the York Hotel on Nicolson Street for the 1863-1864 season, and later in 1870 he used the old Southminster Music Hall as a venue.

In 1866, he took on a season's lease from the Bristol Rifle Drill Hall Company for the use of the Volunteer Rifle Drill Hall on Queen's Road.

Drill Halls were very much a part of nineteenth century military and social life. Initially created for the military drilling of volunteer rifle units, they also became an excellent space for exhibitions, functions, and such-like – including circus. Hengler used the Bristol venue for three seasons between 1866 and 1869. We can get a good impression of how the circus appeared from a report in the *Bristol Times and Mirror* of 27 July 1869;

> For the week past, carpenters, painters, paper-hangers, decorators, etc., have been busy all day long fitting up the hall for the company ... The centre ground space has been allotted to the ring; and from this level all round rises

Bristol Rifle Drill Hall 1867 (Postcard, author's collection)

the seat accommodation. The great gallery, which will accommodate about 1,200 people, is at the Blind Asylum [established in 1793 to train the visually impaired for future employment] end of the hall, with the box for the band at the foot. On either side are entrances for the performers and the fine stud of horses (sixty in number) connected with the establishment. Adjoining these are the pit seats, which are covered with crimson baize. The rest of the circular space is allotted thus – that nearest the ring to the amphitheatre; above are fourteen boxes, to hold seven persons each; admirably suited for those who like to enjoy the performance in a free and easy style. The boxes are handsomely papered and suitably upholstered inside and out, and they are supplied with chairs, as also is the amphitheatre, where provision has been made to prevent the spectators being annoyed by dust from the ring. In addition to the usual gas lights depending from the roof, a large chandelier has been placed in the centre, so that the lighting is all that can be desired; the ventilation of the building is likewise amply provided for. Considerable attention has been given to ornamentation; and the appearance of the hall as a whole is very effective and comfortable. The attendance last night showed that the circus still maintains its repute as a place of resort among all classes of the public.

Earlier in 1866, Hengler also took advantage of the new Curzon Exhibition Hall in the centre of Birmingham. The Hall was inaugurated on 3 March with a performance of Hengler's Grand Cirque Varieté.

> The interior of the Cirque is complete in every respect, capable of accommodating three thousand persons, and the decorations most *recherche*; the magnificent emblematical devices on ceilings, and the heraldic shields, together with the tasteful groupings of flags of all nations, being most historically correct and interesting. The building is illuminated by several large Chandeliers with hundreds of brilliant jets, most artistically arranged. The Stalls, Boxes, Pit, and Gallery have separate approaches; there is also five hundred feet in length of Promenade; and the comfort of the auditory has been most carefully studied, every part of the house being elegantly furnished and splendidly decorated; the Stalls carpeted throughout, and the seats comfortably cushioned, and covered with crimson velvet. (*Birmingham Journal* 3 March 1866)

The *Birmingham Daily Gazette* of 5 March gives a slightly different description that expands upon the above;

> From each side of the building is an awning of various coloured cloth, giving a tent-shaped appearance. From the centre is suspended a large circular gaslight, containing a large number of jets, and immediately under the gallery is a row of gaslights extending round the building, the engraved glasses producing a very pleasing effect. The whole of the gallery is devoted to a promenade, a single row of seats being placed in front. The pit or second-class seats are placed on either side of the building. The stalls are at the front, and are fitted up in a handsome manner, with crimson velvet seats, and the flooring is nicely carpeted. The boxes are arranged at the back of the stalls, and are also comfortably arranged.

Although Hengler's Cirque was housed in a permanent building, such as the Rifle Drill Hall and the Curzon Hall, the circus itself was not permanent. At the end of the season, the interior construction of the circus was dismantled and sold off at auction. For the Birmingham season this was announced in the *Birmingham Journal* of 30 June 1866, where 'The whole of the capital seasoned timber and other materials used in the construction of the above extensive circus ... to be sold by auction.' Presumably it was much more cost effective to sell off the construction materials and then pay for a new construction at the next venue.

In the October, Hengler had moved on to Hull, where he had already constructed another temporary wooden structure in 1864 to house the circus, on Anlaby Road. This site was regularly used by Hengler and redesigned and improved several times. In September 1870 the 'new' circus was described as;

> A very handsome and commodious structure, decorated in admirable taste, conveniently arranged in every class of seats for the comfort of visitors, and having acoustic and ventilating advantages excelled by few public buildings of the same size and character in this country[5].

In 1887 a permanent building was erected on the site in substantial brick, concrete, and plaster with a grand entrance under a portico supported by wooden columns. It was called simply 'The Circus' and continued as a circus venue until 1898. It later became a theatre. By November 1866, Hengler was back in his base in Liverpool for the winter season.

Although Hengler had erected a wood and brick circus on Glasgow Green in Glasgow in 1862, this was removed and auctioned off by the end of the season (McMillan, 2018:107). Another of his 'conversion' circuses was his Grand Cirque housed in the former Prince's Theatre in Glasgow. He opened there in the October of 1867 to much acclaim. As with his previous conversions, no expense was spared in creating a sumptuous palace of entertainment. The *Glasgow Free Press* of 26 October hailed the circus as 'one of the finest in Europe'. The same article went on to give a brief description of the building;

It measures 160 feet by 100, and has three entrances in West Nile Street, the central one being remarkable for illuminations overhead. The Circus is fitted to hold about 3600 persons, and one of the greatest features is the fact that the view of the circle from all parts of the building is uninterrupted. This of itself is no small recommendation. The lighting has been effected in a highly artistic manner, and is so elevated as to make the performances in the circle of the most brilliant character without interfering with the sight of the observers.

Hengler's Circus in Hull c. 1880. It is the large building on the left of the image (Public domain image)

The Grand Cirque provided entertainment in all forms and much was made of the refreshment provision for circus-goers. The *Glasgow Evening Citizen* of 26 October painted this picture;

The large refreshment bar – which runs across the entire breadth of the Circus at the western end of the building, and is about 70 feet long – has been leased by Mr. Pailthorpe ... In addition to the public buffet in question, two private rooms for the accommodation of gentlemen are situated, one at each end of the bar, and, in fact, every arrangement for the orderly and efficient dispensing of requisite refreshment, to preclude the necessity for going outside for it seems to have been provided.

Hengler seems to have realised that the circus going public would require refreshments and capitalised on this by leasing the available refreshment space – another source of income for him. It was also much better to keep his audience within the building during any intermission rather than running the risk of losing them to outside temptations.

By 1883 his lavish shows were outgrowing the existing circus building and visitor numbers continued to be high. McMillan (2018:262) quotes the following attendance numbers for the first week of the season in January 1883;

Monday Jan. 1st	4 performances	11,469
Tuesday Jan. 2nd	3 performances	9,050
Wednesday Jan. 3rd	3 performances	6,559
Thursday Jan. 4th	2 performances	3,990
Friday Jan. 5th	2 performances	2,734
Saturday Jan. 6th	2 performances	3,638

*Hengler's Cirque on Wellington Street, Glasgow 1885 (*Glasgow Herald *6 November 1885)*

Subsequently, in 1885, Hengler moved to newer and grander premises designed by the theatre architect Frank Matcham, near the central railway station on Wellington Street.

Matcham became famous for designing many circus and variety theatre buildings during the latter part of the nineteenth century and into the twentieth century. The new Grand Cirque opened in November 1885. An insert into the *Glasgow Herald* of 6 November 1885 gives us this information;

> The building has been erected of red brick from designs prepared on a pleasing classical model ... The elevation to Wellington Street has a rather imposing façade, with a tower at each end ... The circus has been constructed in every respect in a most substantial manner, and has been fitted up with all the latest improvements that Mr. Hengler's long experience could suggest ... The circus measures 200 by 100 feet, is 60 feet from floor to ceiling, and has accommodation for about 5,000 persons. The stairs are of concrete, the ventilation good, and all the appointments on a satisfactory scale ... A prominent feature of the new house of entertainment is the precautions that have been taken against panic. Some eight or nine exit doors have been advantageously placed in different parts of the building; while a special outlet, 12 feet wide, opening almost directly from the ring, can be used in cases of emergency.

The same article was at pains to point out that the new building had taken only six months to build, and that the contractors had to excavate to a depth of 17 feet below street level in order to establish firm foundations for the walls. Quite an undertaking! The cost of erecting the Cirque, including fittings and decorations was £6,100 (approximately £477,000 today) and the annual ground rent was £671 (approximately £52,500 today)[1]. Hengler had leased the ground for a period of fifteen years and he continued running the Cirque on Wellington Street through to February 1900. After this time the building was taken over by the Royal Italian Circus. In 1904 plans were passed by the Dean of Guild Court for the construction of a large building on the site of the Cirque to be used as a parcels post office[2]. Work was begun almost immediately and the Wellington Street Cirque existed no more.

Hengler's last Cirque in the city was in a former ice-skating rink previously owned by Arthur Hubner on Sauchiehall Street, near to the Glasgow School of Art. He moved there in 1903 and remained until 1924, after which time it became a ballroom and then a cinema. One of the features of this Cirque, as with many of his other Cirques, was that the arena floor could be lowered by several feet and the area flooded with 23,000 gallons of water (approximately 105,000 litres) in 35 seconds[3] so that water spectaculars could be presented. In an interview given to *The Sketch* on 19 December 1894, Albert Hengler spoke at length about his water novelties. At that time, he owned circus buildings in Liverpool, Glasgow, Dublin, and Hull. When asked about where the water idea had come from, he explained that it had come to him in a dream;

> It was during the time that Miss Beckwith was under an engagement with us in Glasgow, doing her swimming act in a tank, and I said to her husband, 'Would it not be possible to give a decent swimming show in a larger tank, and let all the people see how it is done?' I went to bed with that on my mind and I saw the ring full of water in my sleep, as I have described it to you.

With these thoughts in mind, he set to work with his old manager Alfred Powell and produced the first water pantomime for the 1890 – 1891 season at Hengler's Cirque in London, entitled *The Ocean Wave*. However, it is worth noting that Hengler, in his interview, failed to mention the Noveau Cirque which opened in Paris in 1886 with an aquatic circus sensation, although the press notices of the opening of his show did acknowledge the fact;

> ... a form of entertainment that sprang into being a year or two ago at the Noveau Cirque, in Paris ... it is really surprising how speedily and effectively a circus ring can be turned into a real lake sufficiently large to accommodate several rowing boats, a steam launch, and an island, to say nothing of a gigantic frog, personated by a little boy, a flock of real live ducks, and a whole crowd of people who, at the finish, are beheld struggling and creating fun in the water ... The mechanical arrangements ... are so simple as to be actually wonderful. A lining is first laid over the tan circus, upon this a waterproof sheet is so arranged that the ring becomes a gigantic bath, capable of holding some 23,000 gallons of water (approximately 105,000 litres); and, by scenic accessories, admirably and swiftly built up, this becomes a lake with a

practicable island in the centre, with light, picturesque bridges connecting same to the mainland. (*The Era* 3 January 1891)

An illustration in *The Graphic* of 10 January 1891 gives us a clear idea of how the water pantomime may have looked.

THE WATER PANTOMIME AT HENGLER'S CIRCUS

Hengler's water pantomime. The Graphic *10 January 1891 (Author's collection)*

Hengler first opened a Grand Cirque in London in 1871. He acquired the lease on land in Argyll Street on which stood a building formerly known as the Corinthian Bazaar[4]. It was also known as the Palais Royal. Hengler constructed his entirely wooden arena within the shell of the main hall of the Corinthian bazaar. The west wing of the bazaar, with the Corinthian frontage on Argyll Street, was remodelled to form the entrance to the circus. The arena, comprising a circular ring surrounded by stepped seating and a series of private boxes was placed in the north end of the building, leaving ample space for circulation and room at the south end for dressing rooms and stables. A description in *The Era* of 3 September 1871 gives us a clear idea of how it may have looked.

For this purpose he has taken the building which not long since was introduced to our readers under the name of the Palais Royal, situate in Argyll Street, Oxford Circus. This has alternately been the home of talking machines, wizards, panoramas, and kindred exhibitions. Now, however, the whole building has been remodelled, and one of the handsomest, as well as most comfortable, places of amusement in the form of a grand Circus occupies the whole building ... The fashionable folk of the West [end of London] will, when they gain admittance, agree with us that the interior is both elegant and comfortable. It is arranged to accommodate around fifteen hundred visitors ... The auditorium consists of private boxes, handsomely decorated, and affording accommodation for six persons [per box]; luxurious stalls, a roomy pit, and a spacious promenade. The painting of the frieze by Mr. John O'Connor representing "Peace, Mirth, and War", with bas-relief *tableau*, will in itself well repay a visit. The entrances to the building are spacious and convenient, and the ventilation is in every way perfect. The handsome ceiling, pillars, and general decorations reflect great credit on Mr. J. Rorke ... to whose hands the work was entrusted. The upholstery and fittings, too, have been carefully attended to ... Numerous and elegant chandeliers have been supplied by Messrs. W. R. Winfield, of Birmingham, and the whole interior construction has been carried out under the superintendence of J. T. Robinson Esq., architect ... The refreshment department is in the able hands of Messrs. Baylis and Coste, upon whom the pleasure-seeking public may confidently rely for a prompt and good supply of creature comforts. A commendable feature in connection with the building is the fact that all "harpies' fees" are to be "conspicuous by their absence," lavatories, cloak rooms etc., being thrown open free of all charge ... Mr. Hengler ... stated that it was his intention to spare neither trouble, time, nor expense to make his Circus the best in the Metropolis.

Although constructed of wood it was a grand building by any means. However, being of wood it was eventually considered unsafe and by 1884 it was forced to close for redevelopment. The following report describes Hengler's New Grand Cirque that opened in 1885;

... great was the disappointment some twelve months ago when it was discovered that the Board of Works, in their zeal for public safety, had condemned the building, and had for the time being banished from London one of the very best equestrian entertainments it has ever known ... and exceedingly welcome was the news that he had entered into negotiations with the freeholders of the site, and having obtained a long lease, had determined to reconstruct the building ... on an even grander scale than before ... It occupies the same area as formerly, all the entrances being in Argyll Street. There are four wide doorways, giving access, respectively, to the 4s., 3s, 2s., and 1s. parts. Four steps up from the street level and the visitor is on the corridor of the grand tier. This corridor goes completely round the cirque, and there is a corresponding corridor on the lower floor level with the ring and first platform of seats. There is also one tier, called the balcony, on the first floor over the grand tier corridor, so the public have three distinct corridors, on three floors, all round the cirque. At the four angles of the outer square of the site are staircases always open and available. In addition to the four doorways in Argyll Street, there are three exit doors to Marlborough Mews, at the opposite corner, thus giving seven wide exits always open and available. The construction of the cirque is entirely fireproof, the walls are of brick, the staircases and corridors, and the roof over corridors of cement concrete, resting on iron girders embedded in the concrete; and the main roof is of iron, covered with slate, and lined beneath with fibrous plaster. In a similar way all the iron columns which support the circular roof are covered with plaster of Paris, one and a half inches thick, finished of course ornamentally. The roof is one of the largest in London. It is constructed of iron trellis ribs, and is domical in form, with a span of 80ft. The iron drum into which the trellis ribs are fixed is 6ft. diameter, and acts as the ventilating shaft. Under the domed ceiling is a circular cornice, from which spring a series of circular groins, supported by Corinthian columns. The domed ceiling rises in the centre to a height of 46ft. from the level of the ring. The ring is 42ft. diameter, and has two main entrances for the performers and horses. These are right and left, opposite the private boxes, which are in the same position as of the late cirque. The orchestra is on the balcony level, exactly in the centre between the entrances into the ring, and opposite the Royal box. This box occupies the whole space between the supporting columns in the centre of the cirque, and projects slightly. There are five private boxes on either side of the Royal box, all entered from the corridor, level with the entrance in Argyll Street. There are cloak and retiring rooms for both ladies and gentlemen adjacent. Refreshment saloons are also arranged on each floor for every division of the audience. One of the features of Mr. Hengler's establishment has always been the splendid stud of horses. These will now find a permanent home in the rear of the cirque, and the stables, opening out from the corridor, will form not the least attractive part of the establishment. The interior decoration is cream colour and gold, the ceiling being painted in Italian Renaissance ornament in gold and colours. The background of the walls is red, and the curtains and upholstery of crimson velvet. The cirque is lighted by a large central sunlight exactly over the centre of the ring, and by eight hanging chandeliers, which depend all round over the first platform outside the ring-fence, which will give a very brilliant effect. (*The Era* 10 January 1885)

When Charles Hengler died in 1887, the enterprise was taken over by his sons but the circus in London now had stiff competition from rival companies. Finding the running of the Grand Cirque on Argyll Street a costly business, the Henglers leased the circus to Eduard Wulff but by 1895 the circus had closed and the building became the National Skating Palace. A later attempt at running a circus in the building was made in 1905, when the Royal Italian Circus, managed by Signor Volpi, took up residence. Again, competition and a demand for costly improvements became too much to sustain the circus and it had to close. The building on Argyll Street was redesigned by Frank Matcham and became the London Palladium theatre in 1910. The building is still in use today.

Hengler set the vogue for new circus buildings throughout the United Kingdom. He was responsible for building several circus buildings, or adapting existing buildings for circus performances, during the latter half of the nineteenth century. He created circuses in Dublin, London, Bristol, Birmingham, Liverpool, Edinburgh, and Hull. The Henglers, senior and junior, certainly were circus impresarios and it may be thought that they had the monopoly on circus buildings at this time. Influential as they may have been, they were not alone. Other circus owners were equally quick with the erection of circus buildings in wood and stone during the century.

Notes

1. *Glasgow Evening Post* 28 September 1886

2. *Edinburgh Evening News* 16 June 1904

3. *The Glasgow Story*. Online at; TheGlasgowStory: Hengler's Circus

4. British History online at; Argyll Street Area | British History Online (british-history.ac.uk)

5. *Hull Packet* 16 September 1870

CHAPTER 4

BEYOND HENGLER

During the latter part of the nineteenth century many new circus buildings were erected around the country. Some, like the following example[1], were still constructed of wood and yet were as opulent as their stone-built counterparts.

> Mr. James Newsome has opened a circus in the newly erected wooden building, Park Row, opposite the New Theatre Royal. The architect is Mr. J. Hurst … The building has eight sides and each of these goes direct from the top deep into the ground, this giving a very solid foundation. From every one of the eight sides are transept-like projections, and the seating runs up them to the furthermost point, the consequence being no obstruction to those present having a complete view of the arena. Advantage is taken of this mode of construction to obtain stable accommodation for a large number of horses, dressing rooms, and other conveniences … The entrance lobby is 30ft. long by 10ft. wide and 15ft. high … the gasolier in the centre having 3000 glass drops, and there are Prince of Wales plumes in gas jets at the sides. It is stated that about 3000 spectators can be accommodated in the building.

James Newsome was a very popular circus proprietor of the period and constructed many semi-permanent circus buildings around the country to accommodate his circus. Like many of the time, these buildings were decommissioned at the end of the season and the material auctioned off. His circus in Bristol was only used for the summer season May to the end of August before he moved on to Newcastle upon Tyne.

In the August of 1876, the Newcastle Corporation announced that plans had been approved for the erection of a 'handsome and commodious' building for the accommodation of the various circus companies that regularly visited the town[2]. It was to be constructed in a classical style, the front elevation to be of stone with the side elevations to be of brick, fronted with stone. It was designed to replace the temporary wooden buildings that had previously been used by circuses and was envisioned that it would seat around 3000 people. However, the proposal was not welcomed by everyone. In an edition of the *Newcastle Daily Chronicle* of 1 September 1876, the following letter was printed;

> ... praying that such an erection be not constructed, on the ground that it would demoralise the neighbourhood, disturb its peace, and deteriorate the value of property in the vicinity. The plans were then rejected, but have since been modified and passed ... Speaking for myself, I consider, Mr. Editor, that it will be a cruel injustice to me to plant a permanent circus opposite my school gates. If this be done, I cannot hope to carry on my school in the quiet manner I have hitherto done. My pupils will be constantly exposed to temptation, and all sorts of vice and immorality will be presented to them for their imitation. Study in the evenings will be out of the question. If the proposed circus be erected, I shall be constrained to leave the neighbourhood, and break up an old and well-known educational establishment ... to make room for a more questionable institution.

Interesting how some attitudes towards the circus have not changed across the centuries! However, construction work was begun and the new permanent circus opened on 1 May 1878 with none other than Charles Hengler's circus in residence. The following description is given of the building;

> The dimensions of the building are; length 120ft.; width 85ft.; height 44ft. The arrangements of the interior are admirable. While the architects have succeeded in using to the best advantage the large space at their disposal, they have carefully provided for the comfort of the visitors, ensured an uninterrupted view from all parts of the house, and – a matter of the first importance in buildings of this description – have taken care that the means of egress should be easy and abundant. The boxes, which are readily reached, occupy a large space at the Percy Street end of the building. Immediately opposite, and divided by the ring, are two galleries, an upper and a lower; and on either side between the boxes and the galleries are the large divisions of pit and promenade. Strength and substantiality have been aimed at in all the details of the erection, though the elaboration that was intended in

these respects has not yet been wholly carried out. The place is well lighted, and when opened tonight the circus will we are sure present a brilliant and elegant appearance. (*Newcastle Courant* 3 May 1878)

Although the circus was opened on time, it was clearly not finished, as indicated in the above. A slightly earlier report of the building given in a different newspaper was descriptive but not quite as flattering, although honest;

It is a substantial structure of brick, is square in form, and covers a large area. It does not from without give promise of what is to be found within. The front elevation, owing to want of time, has not been completed, only the principal entrance, that leading to the dress circle and private boxes, and which is of stone, having been constructed. It is intended however to erect shops on either side of this main doorway, and these, while being a source of profit to the owners, will contribute greatly to the appearance of the building by forming along its entire length a spacious balcony on which various descriptions of ornamental shrubs could be placed ... Internally neither pain or expense has been spared. The ring is large, the seating comfortably disposed, the lighting cheerful, the decorations chaste, the furnishings costly, and, what is more important – though not always gained, even after paying for admission at the door – a view of the performers can be obtained from every corner. The dress circle abuts the ring ... and it is faced by the orchestra and upper and lower galleries at the opposite end of the building. On each hand are what, by a stretch of fancy, may be called the pits. They are really rows of seats placed one higher than another. ... The galleries, balconies, and roof are supported by ornamental pillars, which, along with strength and durability, lend an air of grace and dignity to the general design. The decorations are in the Italian style ... Light is obtained from upwards of five hundred gas jets, some of which are grouped in the form of "sunlights" suspended from the ceiling, and others are pendant rings around the circus ... Mr. Irving [the builder] has not been able to do all he is wishful to perform in the way of ornamentation on account of the time at his disposal being limited; but there is no doubt that a week or two will see the final embellishments added ... One of the parts which will be much beautified is the principal entrance, though it has already been laid with tile floors, and in other ways rendered pleasing to the eye ... The stabling is in the rear of the premises. It is not yet ready for occupation ... (*Newcastle Daily Chronicle* 30 April 1878)

By 1883, the building was being used more regularly for public meetings, lecture societies, choirs, concerts, and other exhibitions such as panoramas. Circuses did still appear in the building through to 1888, Wilson's Australian Circus being the last one to perform in the building. After this date visiting circuses set up in other areas of the city and the building was redeveloped as the People's Palace Music Hall, opening in 1889. It underwent further refurbishment in 1895 as the Palace Variety Theatre. It was eventually demolished in 1961 to make way for urban development in the Haymarket area.

This appears to have been the fate of many circus buildings. The city of Leeds, in the north of England, hosted many circus companies throughout the nineteenth century. There were twelve different circus sites in the centre of the city that were regularly used for visiting companies[3]. Most of these sites had semi-permanent wooden structures on them but in 1882, it was planned to erect a new brick building for 'equestrian and other purposes' on New Station Street, immediately outside of the railway station. It was to be named the Victoria Amphitheatre and a detailed description of the building was given in *The Era* of 7 October 1882;

> The site selected for the purpose, as a central situation, could not be improved. New Station Street is a new road leading out of Boar Lane ... and was constructed by the North Western and North Eastern Railway Companies for the accommodation of their large and increasing traffic. In fact, it almost forms part of their stations, and is likewise immediately contiguous to the Leeds terminus of the Midland Railway. Trains from the above railways are departing to all the out townships and more distant places up to a late hour at night, and visitors to the circus after the performances can reach them under cover in two or three minutes ... On the top part of the land, which we have described as a cross, the Gallery is erected, and there is an entrance thereto from Wormald's Street, leading direct to Briggate, the principal street. The Box audience will enter from New Station Street, and the patrons of the Pit from Swinegate. The stabling is under that part of

the building; and horses and materials will be brought in from that street, without interfering with the railway passengers, the sloping and natural declivity of the ground being adapted for that purpose. The building will comfortably hold over 2,000 people, and we are in a position to state that every person in the place will have an unobstructed view of the performances in the ring. A spacious promenade round two-thirds of the building will also accommodate a large number of spectators, and ample dressing and retiring rooms are provided. The ring is 42ft. in diameter [the now general standard measurement], and the total height of the building is 48ft. The length is 152ft., and the breadth 56ft. The breadth from New Station Street to the back of the Gallery is 100ft. Private Boxes have been constructed out of three of the arches of New Station Street, and the building from all points of view is both solid and attractive. The decorations throughout are neat and chaste, and great care has been taken to provide for the proper warming and ventilation of the structure. It is needless to add that the authorities, before passing the plans, have taken good care to provide for the safety of the public in case of an alarm of fire or panic of any kind ... It has been contrived that all the doors for the egress of the audience shall open outwards, and, as the entrances to Boxes, Pit, and Gallery are in separate streets, and utterly distinct from each other, there is not only no fear of three streams of people meeting at a dangerous point, but the whole building can be vacated, however overcrowded, in four or five minutes ... The circus is announced to be opened by Mr. Robert Fossett and his great combined company of equestrian and other artistes on the 16th inst.

The fact that the new Amphitheatre was built immediately adjacent to the railway station allowed for ease of access for visitors to the circus from further afield. The building opened to much acclaim on 23 October 1882 with Fossett's Circus in residence. He continued his season through to the April of the following year. After this time, the building appears to have been put to other use. There were exhibitions of boxing, billiard competitions, and music concerts. From being built to house a circus it seems that the circus was strangely absent after 1883. However, circuses did still occasionally perform there, James Newsome being the last recorded in 1887. In February 1888, a notice appeared in the local newspapers for the sale of the entire contents and materials of the Amphitheatre. After this time, the Amphitheatre was shortly demolished to make way for road developments in the area.

In the same year that the Victoria Amphitheatre opened, plans were made for the construction of a new Hippodrome in Leeds. On a site in Cookridge Street there had been semi-permanent structures for several years but now there was to be a new grand civic building. The old circus building was demolished and work began immediately on the new one. It was not completed until 1885 and although initially designed as a hippodrome the plans were altered so that it became a multi-purpose hall to be used for a wide range of events. It could be converted into a hippodrome as was necessary. Its name was changed from the Hippodrome to the Coliseum.

Leeds Coliseum c. 1990 (Author's photograph)

It was designed by William Bakewell[4] and had an ashlar façade with brick to the sides and rear, and a slate roof. The Gothic Revival style frontage had four bays. The central arch was enriched with carved foliage, carved panels above with shields of the principal Yorkshire towns of the day, a large rose window and panelled parapet with a statue of Britannia at the apex. The lower flanking bays had panelled double-doors within the round arch and stained glass in the fanlights, with paired and single round arched stair windows above; 3-light windows with plate tracery and balustraded balcony to the upper floor. The bays were divided by corbelled buttresses with finials.

> The main hall is 116 feet long and 79 feet wide, with two tiers of galleries facing the orchestra and running along the sides. These galleries rest upon strong iron pillars, and are constructed upon the principle of a horizontal arch, which renders them capable of bearing enormous weights. The roof is constructed in one span of wooden flitches and wrought-iron plates bolted together ... The galleries are approached by four fireproof staircases, one at each corner of the building. Particular attention has been paid by the architect in providing adequate means of egress in case of panic, a total door space of no less than 58 feet being arranged for in the plans. At the north part of the building there is a suite of retiring rooms for ladies, and in an apartment adjoining the crush-room, similar arrangements have been made for gentlemen ... The grand staircase from the crush-room to the dress circle also leads to a foyer, 75 feet long by 15 feet wide, which will serve the purposes of a refreshment room for the first tier ... The body of the hall is to be furnished with handsome and comfortable cushioned seats, and the dress circle is to be fitted with swing bottomed chairs ... Electricity is to be the illuminating agent at the Coliseum. In a room under the private road an engine and two dynamos will generate the electricity ... The hall is also to be fitted with auxiliary oil lamps. (*Yorkshire Post & Leeds Intelligencer* 1 July 1885)

What is interesting about the Coliseum is that it is one of the first venues used for circus that embraced the new technology of electricity throughout the building. In 1878, a previous wooden building on the site occupied by Mr. Adams' circus, had used an electric light to illuminate the front of the circus on Cookridge Street and this appears to have been 'for the first time in Leeds'[5].

If Hengler was the predominant impresario of the time, he certainly had competition, especially in Glasgow. Edward Bostock was a menagerie owner who owned possibly the largest menagerie in the country – *Bostock & Wombwell's Menagerie*. Having toured in Scotland several times, he realised that the country had no permanent zoo and that if he could acquire the right premises, it could be a significant commercial investment.

Early in 1897 he accomplished this and The *Eastern Daily Press* of 17 February 1897 reported a statement from Bostock about his new venture;

Having taken a lease of the Olympia, New City Road, Glasgow it is my intention to open the same in May in first-class style as a "Zoo" for Scotland, and with it combine a circus performance. Scotland has for a long time been behind other countries in this respect ... with my previous experience I hope to inaugurate a collection of beasts, birds, and reptiles, that will do credit to any country ... I am in a position to vary the exhibits from time to time, and this gives me an advantage over those who have one resident collection and speculate very little in dealing ... The opening will be under distinguished patronage, and the entire proceeds of the first exhibition and performance will be given to the Western and Royal Infirmaries.

After extensive refurbishment, the Olympia building opened on Wednesday 12 May as the Scottish Zoo and Variety Circus under the patronage of the Lord Provost of the city. Bostock was very astute in the way he planned the venture to provide the 'only permanent place of amusement of its kind in Europe'. The *Northern British Daily Mail* of 12 May goes on to create a colourful scene in which the building had been thoroughly;

CLEARED, FLOORED, PAINTED, DECORATED, AND ILLUMINATED BY ELECTRIC LIGHT, while the entire building is surrounded with Strong Cages for the reception of the Denizens of the Forest. Palms and other Plants, Fountains, &c., have been added, turning the Huge Building at once into a High-Class Educational Institution and ZOOLOGICAL PROMENADE. No more suitable establishment could be opened in Scotland to commemorate the Queen's Diamond Jubilee than the SCOTTISH ZOO ... THE ZOO offers practical opportunities for Zoological research in one of the most complete collections in Britain. THE LIONS, TIGERS, LEOPARDS AND OTHER SAVAGE ANIMALS have been trained to perform in a most remarkable manner, and will serve to illustrate the supremacy of man over the brute creation. CHILDREN WIL BE ABLE TO ENJOY A RIDE UPON THE ELEPHANTS, CAMELS, DROMEDARIES, ZEBRAS &c.

The Zoo was open daily, from 11am until 10.30pm at a charge of one shilling for adults and six pence for children (sixpence for all after 6pm). Performances with the animals were three times a day, and feeding at least once daily. But there was to be more – Bostock combined the ever-popular circus with his zoo. In the centre of the building, he constructed and entirely separate circus venue. Visits to the circus were optional, at the price of two shillings for reserved seats, one shilling pit and promenade (children half price), and sixpence for all classes in the gallery, with three performances a day. It was a permanent circus that drew a wide range of skilled artistes from around the world. Bostock spared no expense and his first season ran unbroken for almost a year. And here was his clever marketing ploy – 'No Person can visit the Circus except those passing through the Zoo'. So, if you wanted to watch the circus you had to pay to see the zoo first!

Five years later in 1902, Bostock went into partnership with a Thomas Barrasford and they redeveloped the Olympia building into the Glasgow Hippodrome. The circus-variety and zoo were now separated, although connected by a corridor. Bostock took sole ownership of the building in 1904 and then went on to build several other Hippodromes in Scotland, including one in Paisley and another in Hamilton. He also bought the *Royal Italian Circus*. In 1919 it was announced that the Scottish Zoo Buildings were being sold and were to become a repair depot and garage. The building now houses a snooker club, a small Chinatown and restaurant, although some of the original iron work can be seen inside.

Glasgow Chinatown c. 2017. The site of the former Hengler's Cirque (Public domain image)

Although Hengler's Grande Cirque in London had become an ice-skating rink by the turn of the century, the new London Hippodrome offered a circus programme once again in the capital. When it opened on the 16 January 1900, it was enthusiastically received;

> A notable addition to Metropolitan places of amusement was made last evening, when the London Hippodrome, the magnificent new building in Leicester Square, was opened. When the electric lights were turned on, a brilliant scene was presented. The house, lavishly decorated in cream and gold, and brilliantly illuminated, was crowded. White bouquets, tied with coloured streamers, were placed in the boxes, and there was every indication that, both in comfort and the quality of the entertainment, everything that money can command would be provided. (*London Evening Standard* 16 January 1900)

The above edition goes on to give in full the details of the circus performance in the arena that night, including an exhibition of wild cats. But it is what happened towards the end of the show that is even more noteworthy, as *The Sketch* of 17 January details;

> The building is not only architecturally and decoratively one of the handsomest places of amusement in London but its mechanical appliances altogether may be classed as the most wonderful to be found anywhere within the Metropolis ... But first a word to the mechanical appliances of the stage. This can be raised *en bloc* three feet from its normal position, or lowered four feet, by a powerful hydraulic ram quite capable of supporting an ironclad [a nineteenth century armour-plated warship], while it can be tilted up from a horizontal position so as to effect a very decided rake, by means of another ram. When sunk to its lowest level, the stage becomes continuous with the arena. This arena, again, may be made to sink, when it is so desired, fully eight feet, thus providing a receptacle capable of holding 100,000 gallons of water (equal to approximately 455,000 litres and 400 tons in weight), in which aquatic sports may be exhibited. The arena is of the usual dimensions – that is forty-two feet diameter – and, by a hydraulic apparatus, a continuous steel railing, twelve feet high, can be raised in the course of a couple of minutes to enclose the arena, when wild beasts are

about to be introduced into the ring. During the time that these changes are being made, the audience is entertained by eight fountains, which raise jets to a great height, and these, illuminated with various coloured limelights, send their sparkling waters towards the roof, while thousands of tiny jets, issuing from a pipe running round the edge of the arena, assist in producing a *mise-en-scène* of marvellous beauty.

The building had been designed by Frank Matcham, one of the over 120 such theatres he designed in his life time, and included cantilevered galleries. In this way the traditional supporting columns could be done away with the ensure that all members of the audience had an unobstructed view of the action. The side entrances to the arena could also be lowered and flooded so as to allow the entry of boats and a sliding roof above the proscenium arch allowed performers to dive into the flooded arena. Water spectaculars were not uncommon, Hengler in particular was very fond of presenting them, but the technological advancements made in the London Hippodrome were, to many, the stuff of dreams.

> The description of the heating and ventilation arrangements reads like a page out of Jules Verne. Drawn in from above the roof, the air passes through an apparatus wherein "dust particles, micro-organisms, and foggy vapour" are removed. If necessary, it seems, "the air can also be disinfected". Having [...] an enormous chamber between the girders of the roof, it is forced down into the auditorium by means of a powerful blowing fan. So, "washed, filtered, and humified" air enters the London Hippodrome ... (*The Daily News* 30 December 1899)

Unfortunately, like many other circus buildings, it had a short life as a circus and became repurposed into a variety theatre in 1909. Although the building can still be seen today, much of the original interior has gone. In 1958, much of the interior was demolished and the building became a nightclub. For a short period of time in 2004 circus made a revival as 'Cirque at the Hippodrome' but this lasted only one year after which time it was converted into a casino.

Advertising poster for Hengler's Cirque in London c. 1871 (Public domain image)

Prior to Hengler opening his Cirque on Argyll Street in 1871, a New Royal Amphitheatre was constructed in High Holborn for Thomas McCollum. *The Era* of 5 May 1871 gave this announcement;

> ... it is with pleasure that we announce to our readers that a most spirited attempt will shortly be made to revive the glories of the peaceful sawdust ring. On the site of the Holborn Horse Bazaar is now rapidly progressing towards completion an Amphitheatre which will vie with any building in London in the beauty and elegance of its decorations, and its admirable arrangements for the safety and comfort of the public ... The building has three entrances. The "Grand" is wide and roomy, and arches are to support the ceiling. Decorations in the Pompeian style are to be used here, and an extremely handsome stone staircase (carved balustrades) leads to the boxes. The corridor at the back is entered through an aperture, which can be closed with steel shutters, and the Amphitheatre will contain twenty-four private

boxes. A balcony follows the circle in front of the boxes, and in it will be placed 200 damask-covered spring seats (numbered and reserved). The pit, which is entered from the west side, is intended to accommodate 500 persons, and here again stuffed seats will be supplied. The gallery, access to which will be made from the east, is arranged to seat 550 persons. The front row will be cushioned and reserved, and, like those lower in the building, will turn back. The curve of the Amphitheatre is extremely imposing, and the ceiling will be constructed of stretched and illuminated canvas, with a large centre flower radiating from the sunlight ... All the entrances are fireproof; and all the staircases of stone; and especial care has been taken to provide facilities for clearing the building in a few minutes, should that necessity ever arise. Ventilation is promoted by an immense air-shaft, which runs through the entire structure ... A crystal sunlight, nine feet in diameter, and containing nine hundred and sixty burners, will illuminate the whole of the auditorium. The supply of water will be copious, hydrants being fixed on every floor. Refreshments will be procurable in the theatre ... At the back of the Pit will be found an enclosed Promenade fifteen feet in width. Iron doors and steel shutters are the rule throughout the establishment. There are two separate sets of stables, and sixteen dressing-rooms, replete with comfort, for the use of the double company of equestrians and dramatic artists.

The amphitheatre opened on 26 May to a full house, with an extensive programme of equestrianism, acrobatic leaping, juggling, and other entertainments.

Much of the activity took place in the ring but a small stage allowed for short dramatic pieces. The performance lasted a full three hours with only one in interval of ten minutes! Full details of the individual acts were given in a report in *The Era* of 26 May 1871. The same report gave a further description of the interior of the amphitheatre that expands on that given above.

The entire span of the theatre ... is seventy-six feet in the clear – the whole length being 130 feet. From box to box the width is sixty feet. In the centre of the house, and facing the stage, is the Royal Box, with an ante-chamber immediately behind ... The arena is 120 feet in circumference [giving a slightly smaller ring than the average 132 feet]. A drop curtain, effectively painted ... and of a classical design, tastefully sets off the proscenium; and the stage, though not very deep, is commodious enough for the light dramatic entertainments which are to be given in conjunction with equestrianism.

*Holborn Amphitheatre 1868 (*The Penny Illustrated Paper *1 February 1868)*

Although Hengler may have dispensed with the stage and concentrated on the action in the arena, it is clear that other circus buildings, such as the Holborn amphitheatre still were built with a stage for 'light dramatic entertainments.' The building was often advertised as the Royal Amphitheatre and Circus or the Royal Amphitheatre and Cirque, or sometimes simply as the Holborn Amphitheatre. As we have seen with other circus buildings, the entertainments offered began to be less circus and more choral and dramatic, as well as being a space for public meetings. In 1875, the building underwent some reconstruction and opened as a 'cheap drama, ballet, and opera house'[6]. By March 1876, it had been converted into a roller-skating rink and then back to a theatre once more the following year. In 1879. Its name was changed to the Connaught Theatre and its connection with circus finally severed. The building survived until the second World War, when it was damaged by bombing. It was subsequently demolished.

The second half of the nineteenth century saw a surge of circus activity. Circus buildings began to appear in many major towns and cities around the country, and not all of them at the behest of Hengler. Some lasted for only a relatively short period, others for longer, but they all gave witness to the popularity of the circus at that time.

Notes

1. *The Builder – An illustrated Weekly Magazine*. Vol.34 p519. 27 May 1876 (1)

2. *Ibid.* Vol.34 p817. 19 August 1876

3. Ward. S. (2021) *The Victorian Circuses of Leeds.* Amazon

4. *Revised Listed Buildings; City of Leeds*. Vol.1 A-F. Dept. of National Heritage 1996

5. *Yorkshire Post & Leeds Intelligencer* 6 November 1878

6. *Illustrated Sporting and Dramatic News* 2 January 1875

CHAPTER 5

FROM BRIGHTON TO BLACKPOOL

Another permanent, although relatively short lived, circus to make its appearance in 1876 was that of circus proprietor John Ginnett. Ginnett's father had been a Napoleonic prisoner of war after the battle of Waterloo in 1814. Electing to remain in Britain at the end of the war, he began presenting a pony and budgerigar act. This was the humble beginning of the Ginnett circus dynasty. When John Ginnett moved to Brighton, on the south coast of England, in 1876, he began the erection of a circus building. It was constructed of brickwork, with a roof of wood and iron. It was 50 feet in height, 80 feet wide, and 120 feet long with a ride (arena) of 150 feet in circumference. The promenade exceeded 200 feet. The décor was in gold and crimson and the whole illuminated by 1000 gas jets. The boxes and stalls could seat 300, and the pit 1500. Another 1500 could be accommodated in the gallery. It was said to have been built in the style of the Cirques in Paris and Madrid. What is interesting is that in the report given in *The Builder*[1] it gives some indication of the cost of this building. The purchase of the land was given as £1000 – and the building costs £4000. The total cost of £5000 would have an approximate equivalent today of £331,000; a significant amount of money to invest in a building that would become the Gaiety Theatre a few years later in 1890.

Ginnett toured two circus outfits at this time but in 1891, at a cost of £13,000, he opened another stone-built circus which he named the Hippodrome. In the press (*The Era* 24 November 1891) its dimensions were given as being 80 feet by 150 feet and it could hold 5000 people. There were eight private boxes, and a carpeted lounge of 70 feet in length. The height from floor to roof was 50 feet. An eye-witness account of the time[2] reported that the interior had a 42 feet (13 metres) diameter inner ring with a 60 feet (18 metres) diameter outer ring. The outer ring could be submerged in fifty seconds to form a lake with the central ring as an island.

Sadly, Ginnett died in the January of 1892 and the Hippodrome was taken over by his son Albert. The building became the Grand Theatre in 1904 and eventually closed in 1955. It was destroyed by fire in 1961.

There is another Hippodrome that can be seen today in Brighton. It is in Middle Street and originally began life as an ice-skating rink in 1897. Despite ice-skating being a Victorian vogue, this was not a successful venture. The rink was developed into a circus in 1901, designed by that renowned theatre architect Frank Matcham. The existing frontage, bearing the name Hippodrome, although now sadly dilapidated, remains very much as it would have been in its early days.

Exterior view of the Brighton Hippodrome (Courtesy of David Fisher)

Matcham installed a circus ring in the centre of the auditorium with seating arranged in a horse-shoe around it. To one side of the ring, opposite the foyer entrance, he added a stage with a proscenium arch. On either side of the stage were equestrian entrances accessed from the outside by equestrian ramps. The interior was decorated largely in white encrusta (a deeply embossed wall covering) with plaster embellishments. The domed roof was tent like and was also white, reflecting the electric lights within the building.

The Era 25 May 1901 gave a description of the Hippodrome;

Interior view of the Brighton Hippodrome c.1900 (Courtesy of David Fisher)

The ground floor is provided with raised stepped seating continuing all round to the entries of the ring, and the entire portion is divided for the highest priced patrons. Private boxes are arranged along the back with open lounges at the two ends, commanding a perfect view of the ring and stage. The side seats have a splendid view, and at the rear are wide, handsome promenades. Over the ground floor is a fine large balcony built on the cantilever principle, and this is set far enough back and with an easy rake so that the seats command a good and uninterrupted view. A wide promenade is continued around the whole of the balcony.

Sadly, because of the financial ineptitude of the owner, the Hippodrome closed as a circus the next year, in 1902, and was then converted into a variety theatre. It remained as a variety theatre until 1967. Lord John Sanger's Circus appeared there in 1934 and the last circus to appear at the Hippodrome was in 1947. From 1967 to 2006 it functioned as a Bingo Hall. Now it has been designated as a Grade 3 Listed Building and is #1 on the Theatres Trust list of 'Theatres at Risk'. The building is currently undergoing restoration and the initial work is a new roof being constructed over the existing roof so as to preserve the original structure. Preservation work can then begin on the interior and the ultimate plans are for the Hippodrome to be revitalised as a multi-purpose performance venue.

As well as having a permanent base in Brighton, the Ginnett circus toured widely throughout the country, erecting temporary structures where they performed. As early as the 1860s it was appearing in Belfast, Northern Ireland, erecting its circus at various places such as the Botanic Gardens and on New Market. It was not until the 1880s that Ginnett had a more permanent circus in that city. In fact, it was down to a rival company belonging to Mr. Harmston that the first 'permanent' structure was built. In 1882 it was reported in the press that;

> Among the many improvements at present in progress in Belfast, a new permanently constructed circus, now being erected in Glengall Place, will undoubtedly be looked upon by a large section of the public as a most desirable addition to the places of amusement already in existence. The site chosen is the large vacant plot of ground beside the Great Northern Railway terminus, and the new building will be replete with all the latest improvements and novelties known in circus construction. Throughout its entire area the edifice is substantially strengthened with massive wood and iron girders and braces. The felting of the roof is being carried out on a new and improved principle, whereby it will be rendered weather-proof and durable. The principal entrance in Glengall Place will consist of a grand vestibule, twenty feet wide, from which will spring staircases to the pit and also to the promenade, which is intended to run entirely around the building. At the opposite end, and in Glengall Street, is the gallery entrance, and on which side are two spacious means of exit to be used in case of emergency. The seating capacity of the circus is estimated at three thousand, and the arrangements in stalls, boxes, pit, and gallery are such as to ensure the comfort and convenience of the audience. The lighting will be on a new plan, whilst the decorative work is to be carried out in the most tasteful manner, and altogether beyond what is generally seen in establishments of the sort. (*Belfast News-Letter* 3 November 1882)

Like many circuses constructed during this period, emphasis was made upon the ease of exit in cases of emergency. Fire, as we have seen, was an ever-present danger in places of entertainment that were constructed wholly or partly from wood. Proprietors of circus buildings were keen to reassure their visitors that they would be safe when watching their circus. Another feature of this circus in Belfast is that it was built on land adjoining a railway station. This made access to the circus much easier for visitors from outside of the city. You may recall that the Victoria Amphitheatre in Leeds, also built in 1882, had the same facility.

After 1882, the building appears to have been used for many different activities but no circuses were advertised there. Around 1885, Ginnett took over the building and adapted it for his own use. He presented a winter season there as Ginnett's Hippodrome and Circus until 1887, when the building was remodelled and improved to hold 4000 people, and became known as Ginnett's Olympia Hippodrome and Circus, but shortened very quickly to Ginnett's Olympia.

And why Olympia? It seems from a report in the press[3] that Ginnett adopted the title after a performance attended by Queen Victoria in March 1887 in Brompton, London. Ginnett's Olympia continued until 1894 when it was demolished.

Ginnett's Olympia, Belfast c.1885 (Courtesy of the Grand Opera House and Cirque)

In December 1895 the Cirque and Grand Opera House was opened under the management of J. Warden, with the building designed by Frank Matcham, in an oriental style. Warden became the manager of both the new Cirque and the Theatre Royal under the trading name of Warden Limited. A detailed description of the Cirque building was given in the *Belfast Weekly News* of 14 December 1895;

> The design adapted is Flemish. The architect (Mr. Frank Matcham, of London) has succeeded in treating the elevations in a most artistic manner, the quaint gables, balustradings, and minarets giving quite a Continental appearance to the building. The Glengall Street front has an imposing centre façade, flanked with square towers[4], crowned with boldly moulded and domed minarets ... the building can be used for a circus performance at any time, the architect having by an ingenious arrangement designed a sinking stage, whereon the usual arena can be arranged ... the whole building will be illuminated by the electric light, and with the beautifully painted and

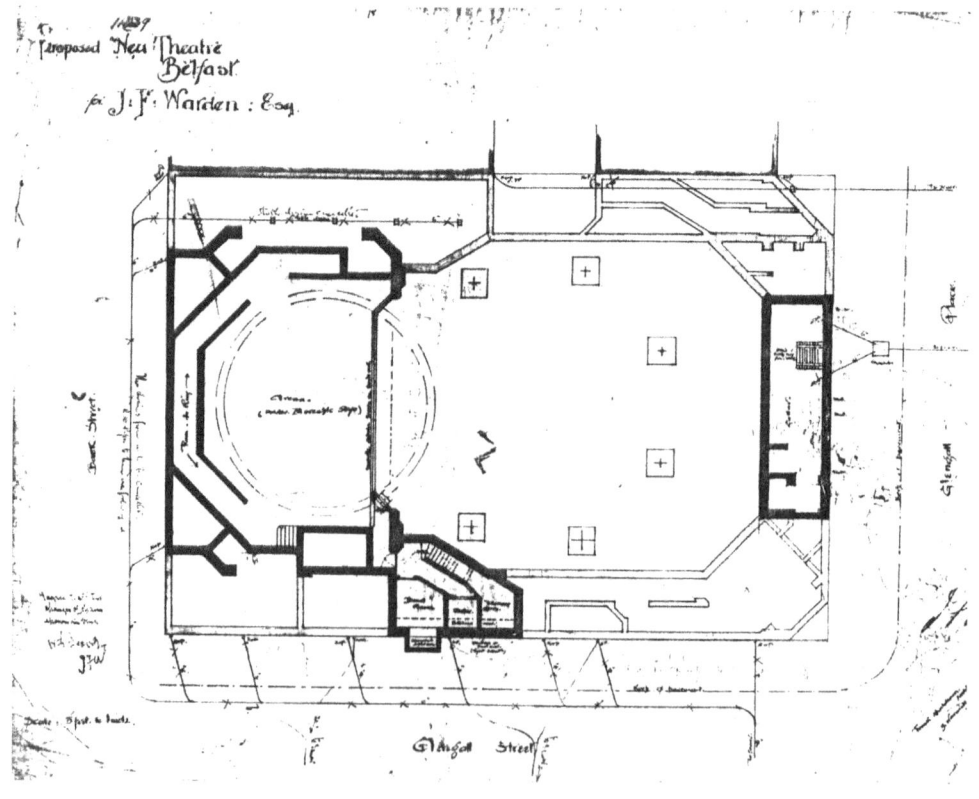

Floor plan of the Grand Opera House and Cirque, Belfast c. 1894, showing the positioning of the circus arena
(Public domain Letter and plans of Frank Matcham to Belfast City Council. Linen Hall Library Belfast)

coloured glass introduced into the windows and shelter a very brilliant and striking effect will be obtained.

The Northern Whig of 17 December gives a little more information;

The building is one of the finest and most extensive in the United Kingdom, and it is estimated will accommodate 3,500 persons. It is situated in one of the most central positions in Belfast, adjoining the terminus of the Great Northern Railway, and the tramway cars pass the doors from all parts of the city. The building stands on a plot of ground measuring 130ft. x 89ft., and is held forever, under fee-farm grant, at the very low rent of £150 per annum ... By a simple mechanical contrivance, and without disturbing any of the seats in the auditorium, the Theatre can within a few hours be converted into a Grand Circus ... There are separate exits from each part of the House, and there are no less than three wide exits from the pit alone. The entire building is fireproof so far as human ingenuity could make it so, and the

Interior scene at the Grand Opera House and Cirque, Belfast c. 1897 (Courtesy of the Grand Opera House Belfast)

stage is entirely separated from the auditorium by substantial walls and a fireproof asbestos curtain. The building is heated with hot-water apparatus and lighted with electricity throughout.

The auditorium was embellished with depictions of various Hindu gods and elephant heads and much of the original decoration still exists today. A contemporary image shows the circus ring set within a proscenium arch, with the audience mostly facing the ring rather than surrounding it.

From the image it does seem that some members of the audience were seated at the rear of the ring. However, having visited the theatre and looked at the available stage space it does seem more likely that what is seen in the image is actually a set construction. There would not be enough space to accommodate an audience to the rear of the stage and such a set would give the illusion of the arena being surrounded by people. The extract from the *Northern Whig* above states that the stage could be lowered mechanically to create an arena. In a letter to the Belfast City Council, Frank Matcham outlines his plans for the new building and mentions the stage arrangement, although no mention is made of any mechanical devices;

> The building is designed with the view for its adaptation for a Circus or Theatre: the Stage therefore will be made moveable, the floor being formed in squares and carried on framed bearers, which when removed, will give space for the fitting up of an Arena for Circus performances. The seating of the Auditorium will not be interfered with, but will remain unaltered for either performances. (*Linen Hall Library Belfast*)

In 1904 the building was renamed the Palace of Varieties and then in 1909 the Grand Opera House. Although much more of a Variety Theatre, circuses continued perform in the building with the last recorded circus being Chapman's Colossal Continental Zoo – Circus in 1934. The building, although now extended and modernised, still retains much of its original opulence and has recently undergone refurbishment and still operates as a performance venue, and is the only building as such in Britain to retain the appellation 'Cirque' on its façade.

Grand Opera House and Cirque, Belfast as it appears today (Author photograph)

Matcham may have designed many theatre buildings throughout his career, including several that accommodated circuses. However, prolific as he was, he was not responsible for the two purpose-built circus buildings that are still in use today in Britain, although he did have a hand in the refurbishment of one of them.

Blackpool Tower is an iconic structure that is situated in the seaside town of Blackpool on the west coast of Lancashire, in England. The 500 feet high structure can be seen from miles around and was modelled on the Eiffel Tower in Paris. Sir John Bickerstaffe, a local Blackpool businessman, had visited the 1889 *Exposition Universelle* in Paris at which the Eiffel Tower was the main attraction. He decided that Blackpool should have its own tower. Although construction work, under the auspices of the Blackpool Tower Company, began in 1891 there had been a place of amusement on the site since 1873; *Dr. Cocker's Aquarium, Aviary, and Menagerie.* The newly planned Blackpool Tower was to embrace this and crown a leisure complex that included the aquarium, aviary, and menagerie, as well as a ballroom, and a salon. The Menagerie continued in operation until 1973 and the Aquarium finally closed in 2010. The complex was designed by two architects, James Maxwell and Charles Tuke, although neither lived to see the opening in 1894. The estimated cost of the construction was £290,000 (approximately £237,794,300 today). Situated between the base of the four legs of the tower was built a circus; the world-famous Blackpool Tower Circus. It opened on 14 May 1891 to much acclaim, with an entry price of six pence (6d.)

It would seem that no popular holiday resort can be thoroughly equipped for the delectation of visitors without an Eiffel Tower. The proposal to erect such a Jacob's ladder at Blackpool has taken very practical shape, and some particulars are at hand of the structure ... It will be almost rectangular in form, with a tower 100ft square in the centre. The base of this is to be used as a circus, with four entrances, besides performers and horse entrances. On the right and left of the circus are large arcades for the sale of toys, jewellery, and other fancy articles. The outside portion of the ground floor, facing the three principal streets, will be devoted to shops.

The heart of the first floor will be occupied by the circus gallery, and the remainder of the floor by the menagerie and aquarium, to which will be added on this floor an attractive waxwork exhibition, and by popular exhibitions of varied kinds. The second floor will be a spacious promenade, concert room, and floral hall, with an area of nearly 30,000 square feet, with two storeys of open-air balconies and cafés facing the sea. The basement will be partially occupied by the circus with the various waiting rooms for the equine and human performers, and partly by the boilers, engines, dynamos, and pumps for the electric lighting and passenger lifts, and for other administrative purposes. (*Liverpool Mercury* 13 June 1891)

The circular pit seating was arranged in tiers and rose up to a pit promenade. This was backed by more elevated seats and completed with four galleries that were brought together in a square. This allowed for an unrestricted view of the arena from all sections of the house. The accommodation was for 5000 spectators. The original interior design had an oriental focus;

Decorations were orientally inspired with numerous Japanese landscapes and seascapes painted onto canvas and fixed to the walls ... Pagoda shaped canopies draped the ring entrances, oriental lanterns hung from the ceilings and even the ring staff wore kimonos and black pigtails. (Sheward & Potier, 1990:4)

The original layout of the arena provided seating for approximately 2500 persons, although today it seats nearer 1600. The floor to ceiling height was initially 43 feet but has since been reduced to 35 feet after the introduction of a modern lighting rig.

By 1899 it was refurbished under the design of Frank Matcham. Bouissac (2022)[5] likens it to a temple or pagoda. The new design was now in the Moorish Alhambresque style;

Interior view of Blackpool Tower Circus (Late C19th postcard. Author's collection)

The vestibule floors and walls were treated with white and red Italian marbles, pendentives were widely applied to the ceilings. The seating was renewed in a new layout, creating a promenade around the top, with a vaulted ceiling in rich calligraphic detail. Spanish tiles in coloured squares were used for the walls of the promenade ... Deep reed drapery was used throughout and the decoration, as now, was a cream base with ruby and green inserts and gold highlights. (Sheward & Potier, 1990:6)

The interior of the circus radiated opulence, with its dark red draperies and gold embellishments. The circus maintained an intimacy, with many seats being at the most only 80 feet away from the centre of the arena. The circus as seen today is still very much as Matcham created.

The Tower Circus originally advertised itself as an 'Aquatic and Variety Circus' due to the construction of a hydraulically operated sinking ring. Often performed at the end of a show, the ring could be lowered six feet and filled with 40,000 gallons of water (approximately 182,000 litres) in approximately two minutes. It was a complex process, as described here;

> Operation is from a single 18 and a half inch diameter hydraulic ram set in a sump at the centre, working from pressure created from a pump. The ram is capable of displacing 40 tons deadweight. The table, or ring floor, which weighs 14 tons, has to be first lifted from its rest position, turned to clear its seating, before pressure on the centre ram is released and the weight of the water entering forces the table down. The tank, which is constructed of glazed brick, takes 8 hours to fill from empty and is drained down at the end of each season. Also included in the original timber ring fence [now made of concrete], as well as the built-in fountains, was a 12 feet high steel ring cage, in two halves, used until about 1948. This was simply hoisted from its housing, swung into the ring, and the two pieces strapped together. (Sheward & Potier, 1990:4)

The hydraulically operated sinking ring was an innovation for British circus, although water spectaculars had been presented by Ginnett and Hengler in previous years. It was not however the first of its kind as the Blackpool system was modelled on that of the Nouveau Cirque in Paris, inaugurated in 1886. The Blackpool ring is only one of four such sinking rings still in use in Europe today. One of those is at the Great Yarmouth Hippodrome, on the east coast of Norfolk in Britain.

As the popularity of Blackpool as a seaside resort grew on the west coast of Britain during the latter part of the nineteenth century, so too did that of Great Yarmouth in the east. Like Blackpool, earlier visiting circuses had set up semi-permanent structures in which to entertain the seaside crowds. George Gilbert, a circus promoter, already had a well-appointed[6] wooden building in the town in 1898 but this was demolished in 1902 to make way for the present Hippodrome, which opened for business on 20 July 1903[7]. R. Scott Cockrill was the locally born architect responsible for the design.

The Yarmouth Hippodrome stands upon a large plot of ground recently occupied by the circus, and a number of shops and private houses, the whole of which have been cleared away to make room for Mr. George Gilbert's enterprising venture ... Mr. Gilbert's intention in building the Hippodrome is to provide Yarmouth with a building equal to any of its kind in the country, and surpassing anything to be found at any other seaside resort with the exception only of Blackpool, a building in which huge water carnivals and scenic displays can be carried out with ease and success ... The fine frontage faces the Marine Parade, and is over 100 ft. in length, and is treated in the free style of the Renaissance in terra cotta and red brick. There are five entrances under the four towers which form so conspicuous a feature of the building; these towers are placed at regular intervals with a large semi-circular arch thrown between each pair. The outside ornamentation is in low relief, the central entrance being flanked by handsome columns. The main entrance is 30ft. by 20ft., and has a beautiful mosaic paved floor. This entrance is enclosed by massive doors, and will be used as a crush and retiring room by those occupying the stalls. (*Norfolk News* 18 July 1903)

Great Yarmouth Hippodrome c.1922 (Postcard. Author's collection)

A major feature of the Hippodrome, like at Blackpool, was the sinking ring that allowed for water spectaculars. The system is still as constructed in 1903 except for the mechanism of lifting the ring floor back into place. The current owner, Peter Jay, gave this explanation;

> The water works like this. Most of it is under the [ring] floor at all times, filtered and chemically treated all year round, heated to 86 degrees [Fahrenheit = 30 Celsius] only when shows are on, heated by electricity. There used to be an old boiler with [a] chimney near the tank that Billy Russell [a former owner] used to burn all the ice cream cartons. We didn't go that way when we restored it. The water is below the floor just below all the massive metal structure, the rest of the water is in the original tank at the top of the south side ramp to the circus ring. When we drop it [the floor] ... there's an original valve we let go at the bottom of the tank. The water flows down into the ring and comes up just over the wooden floor. This takes some of the weight off the rams holding it up ... This gives us about two inches of water over the floor, we often use this as a dance setting or, as last summer, a Cyr wheel act which is very effective in two inches of water ... At this point we have four levers spaced around the edge. There are also two in the centre which we pull during the interval. The last four are then pulled on a whistle signal. They must be pulled together and then the floor drops down the channels, all of which takes about 30 seconds. The only thing changed from this 1903 triumph of British engineering is how we get it back up after the show. We have four heavy steel tripods we bring in after the show and we winch up four big Tirfors [a type of winch]. It takes about 20 minutes to get it all back, the rams pushed back in, and carpets back. Afterwards, the water is pumped back [to the tank] by a large electric motor. About two or three feet depth of water goes back to the tank, the rest stays under the floor.[8]

What is significant about the Great Yarmouth Hippodrome is that it is the only stand-alone permanent circus building in Great Britain still in regular use today as a circus venue. The Blackpool Tower circus is part of a larger building complex and others, such as the Belfast Cirque and Grand Opera House, or the Brighton Hippodrome have either been repurposed or undergoing renovation.

For all that Great Britain may have been the cradle of the circus, no more permanent structures dedicated to circus were built in the country. If circus was so popular then we must ask the question, why? In their 1990 work, Sheward & Potier present us with this rationale;

> Where the lesson has not been learned and worse still, the size of the tent [or amphitheatre] swamps the seating and the show ... Maybe all this explains why so very few circus buildings remain and only those with a capacity of between 1300 – 2000. In general, buildings with capacities on either side of these two extremes have either found it uneconomic to put on a reasonable show or too many patrons have gravitated to the cheaper seats and been disgruntled and never returned.

It is an interesting hypothesis that calls into question the underpinning importance of the 'intimacy' effect in the circus. Is there a critical point at which both the optimum size of the audience and/or the auditorium has an effect upon the nature of the circus performance given and the overall audience experience? This is a debate which will be returned to later in the work.

If the Great Yarmouth Hippodrome was the last permanent dedicated circus to be built in Britain, it is to continental Europe that we must now look for further evidence of grand and opulent permanent circus buildings.

Notes

1. *The Builder* Vol 34. P984. 7 October 1876

2. John Frederick Ginnett (1826 – 1892) – Discover (brightonmuseums.org.uk

3. *Belfast News-Letter* 11 November 1887

4. A central imposing entrance flanked by two towers was a common feature of Matcham's circus theatre designs

5. Bouissac, P. (January 2022) The Otherness of Circus Space; When the circus entered history. *International academic conference address Budapest; Circus Buildings in Europe.* Unpublished address transcript

6. *Eastern Evening News* 26 July 1898

7. *Norfolk News* 25 July 1903

8. Barltrop, C. (January 2021) Circus Buildings in Great Britain. *International academic conference address Budapest; Circus Buildings in Europe.* Unpublished address transcript

CHAPTER 6

THE FRENCH CONNECTION

In Chapter 1 it was mentioned that Philip Astley took his troupe to Paris. It was as early as 1772 that he performed equestrian acts before Louis XV at Versailles. But this was only a short-lived visit and after an extensive period touring Europe in 1782, in which he visited many countries;

> In my travels, taking Brussels, Vienna, etc., in my road to Belgrade, in 1782, I had the honour to be introduced (by sending my name to the professor), to every principal Manège in those countries, Sir Robert Murray Keith, then Minister Plenipotentiary at the court of Vienna, did me the honour of introducing me to the Emperor.[1]

He and his company visited Paris where they gave a command performance before the king and queen. Although it was his teenage son John who was feted by Queen Marie-Antoinette, this visit enabled Astley to give a series of open-air exhibitions in the Boulevard du Temple, not far from the Place de la République today. Henri D'Alméras in *La Vie Parisienne* (1909) writes;

> Le 7 juillet, 1782, l'Anglais Astley avait ouvert sur le boulevard du Temple un Spectacle au Amphithéâtre équestre.

> [On the 7 July, 1782, the Englishman Astley had opened an Equestrian Show or Amphitheatre on the Boulevarde du Faubourg. *Author's translation*]

Astley and company returned to Paris in 1783. It had long been his intention to open an amphitheatre there and now that he had the patronage of the French royal court it seemed an opportune time. He acquired a vacant building at No. 24 Rue du Faubourg du Temple, not so far away from where he had given his open-air performances some years earlier. There he established the Amphithéâtre Anglais and he opened in the November.

It was the first permanent dedicated circus space in Paris, although largely constructed of timber. A description of the new amphitheatre and a taste of the entertainment provided is given in *Histoire des Chevaux Célèbres*, edited and published by P.J.B.N. in Paris 1821;

> C'était un manége spacieux, couvert d'un plafond élégant, et dont la circonference était garnie du plusieurs rangs des loges peintes et décorées. Vingt-huit ou trente candélabres garnis, du plusieurs lampes en verres du couleurs, formant environ douze cents mèches, l'éclairaient d'une manière pittoresque. Au milieu était un théâtre destiné, dans les intervalles des exercices des chevaux, à faire des tours de force très-variés. Aux deux côtés étaient les écuries. Dans le haut était placé l'orchestre ... On distinguait Astley père et fils et deux Anglais. Les chevaux partageaient à juste titre le mérite de ces exercices par l'intelligence la plus étonnante ... Les sieurs Astley executaient, avec des grâces infinite, un menuet à cheval ... Le cheval qui rapportait était fort applaudi; après qu'on le lui avait jeté, il prenait un

Advertising image for the 1784 season at Astley's in Paris (Bibliothèque nationale de France)

mouchoir dans ses dants, l'apportait, sans que les coups de chambrière qui cinglaient à ses oreilles par-vinssent à l'intimider L'attitude du cheval assis, comme un chien, est la plus difficile; il faut qu'il ai les pieds de derrière recourbés, ainsi que ceux de devant, et que le sabot soit appuyé sur le sol: le cheval d'Astley prenait cette attitude si difficile, au commandement de son mâitre.

[It was a roomy manége, covered with an elegant ceiling, and the circumference of which was furnished with several rows of painted and decorated boxes. Twenty-eight or thirty candelabra, furnished with a number of lamps in colored glasses, weighing about twelve hundred pounds, illuminated it in a picturesque manner. In the middle was a theatre destined, in the interludes of the exhibitions of the horses, to make very varied creations. On both sides were the stables. At the top was the orchestra ... Astley father and son and two Englishmen were distinguished. The horses rightly shared the merit of these exhibitions with the most astonishing intelligence. The Astleys executed a minuet with infinite grace, and on horseback... The horse, which was returning, was much applauded; After it having been thrown to him, he took a handkerchief in his teeth, brought it, without the efforts of a waiter who was shouting in his ears, to intimidate him. The attitude of the horse, sitting like a dog, is the most difficult. It must have the curved hind feet, as well as those in front, with the hoof resting on the ground. Astley's horse took such a difficult attitude at the command of his master. *Author's translation*]

Social tensions across France had been increasing for some time and on July 14 1789 the Bastille prison in Paris was stormed by the revolutionary mob. Subsequent events of the French Revolution meant that Astley could not operate his usual winter season in Paris for some time. His focus now became Dublin and London. When war was eventually declared on revolutionary France in early 1793, Astley had little option but to close down his Paris venture and he leased his amphitheatre to Antonio Franconi, who had been working for him for some years. Some accounts imply that he actually sold the property to Franconi;

En sa qualité d'Anglais, Astley avait du fuir au moment dù coalition européenne contre la France; Franconi qui s'intitulait citoyen de Lyon, gagna Paris aussitôt après la destruction de son cirque et acheta l'amphithéâtre équestre d'Astley 21 mars 1793. (*Les Théâtres du Boulevard du Crime* 1905. BNF)

[As an Englishman, Astley had to flee at the moment of a European coalition against France; Franconi, who was a citizen of Lyons, returned to Paris immediately after the destruction of his circus and bought the equestrian amphitheater of Astley on 21 March 1793. *Author's translation*]

Astley may have founded the idea of circus in Britain and had brought the circus to France but it was the Franconi dynasty who would make Paris the European centre for circus in the nineteenth century. It was in 1783 that the Franconi family, Antonio and his two sons Laurent and Henri, had their first association with Astley. They then returned to Lyon, where Franconi established a circus, only to be later destroyed by fire. The purchase of Astley's establishment in 1793 gave Franconi a permanent foothold in Paris. His first move was to build a larger circus in the grounds of the former grounds of the Capucine monastery; Franconi's Circus. In 1805, the elderly Antonio handed over the running of the circus to his two sons and because of redevelopment in the area a new circus was constructed; the Cirque Olympique in honour of the Emperor Napoleon Bonaparte. The new circus was constructed between the rue du Mont-Thabor and the rue Saint Honoré and was opened on the 28 December 1807. This building was the first in France, indeed the world, to have the name of 'Cirque' attached to it.

Le bâtiment est baptisé *Cirque Olympique*. Pour la première fois en France, le terme de Cirque désigne ce modèle d'architecture. (Dupavillon, 1982:67)

[The building is called the Cirque Olympique. For the first time in France the word Circus describes this architecture style. *Author's translation*]

A detailed description of the Cirque Olympique was given by Donnet (1821), a precis of which is given here;

Le cirque, bâti par l'architecte Guinet ... formait originairement dans son ensemble un rectangle ... de deux cents pieds de longeur cent de large ... Sa façade, très insignifiante donne sur un passage couvert qui va de la rue Saint-Honoré à celle du Mont-Thabor. Ce passage qui n'a pas neuf pieds de large, est pourtant le seul débouché public de ce théâtre. Le vestibule, extrêmement resserré, donne accès à trois escaliers très étroits; celui du milieu conduit à l'amphithéâtre et dans l'arène, et par deux retours dans le corridor qui dessert toutes les loges de cet amphithéâtre, et de là au foyer qui régne au-dessus du vestibule; les deux autres escaliers mènent aux seconds et aux troisièmes loges. Le périmètre extérieur de la salle est un polygone régulier de dix-huit côtés, dont cinq sont occupés par l'ouverture de la scène. L'apothème de ce polygone est dequarante-sept pieds, et sa traverse totalede quatre-vingt-quatorze. Sur deux cercles concentriques s'élève une double colonnade de quatorze colonnes très déliées, qui laissent dans l'intérieur une arène de cinquante-deux pieds de diamètre comme celle dé l'ancien cirque. Un amphithéâtre à six gradins, est compris entre les deux colonnades au-dessus, entre lé deuxième rang de colonnes et le périmètre régnent deux étages de galleries partagées chacune en quarante-cinq loges, dont les neuf du fond sont séparées par un petit ordre de pilastres et grilles comme celles de l'avant-scène. Les devantures de loges sont décorées de draperies, les soffites de la galerie circulaire le sont de couronnes. La corniche architrave qui règne sur la colonnade, porte la calotte de la salle, où l'on a figure un rang de loges en voussure qui n'existepas. La hauteur de la salle est de trente-trois pieds. Douze cents spectateurs tiennent dans les loges et l'amphithéâtre, et huit cents assis au parterre qui se garnit de banquettes au bésoin ... Enfin, ce cirque est regardé comme plus vaste que celui d'Astley à Londres.

[The circus, built by the architect Guinet ... was originally formed on a rectangular plot ... two hundred feet long and one hundred wide ... Its façade, very insignificant, overlooks a covered passage running from rue Saint Honoré to rue Mont-Thabor. This passage, not nine feet wide, is the only public access to the theatre, leading to the amphitheatre and the arena, and by two turns into the corridor which serves all the boxes, and from there to the foyer which is situated above the vestibule; two other staircases lead to the second and third boxes. The outer perimeter of the hall is a regular polygon with eighteen sides, five of which are taken up by the opening of the stage. On two concentric circles rises a double colonnade of fourteen very slender columns, which leave in the interior an arena fifty-two feet in diameter, like that of the old circus [seemingly significantly larger than the standard Astleian forty-two feet diameter arena]. A six-tiered amphitheatre is comprised between the two colonnades above; between the second row of columns and the perimeter is situated two floors of galleries each divided into forty-five boxes, the nine of which at the bottom are separated by a small order of pillars and grilled like those of the front stage. The box façades are decorated with draperies; the soffits of the circular gallery are crowned. The height of the auditorium is thirty-three feet. Twelve hundred spectators can fit in the boxes and amphitheatre, and eight hundred seated on the floor which is furnished with benches if need be ... Finally, the circus is considered larger than that of Astley in London. *Author's translation*]

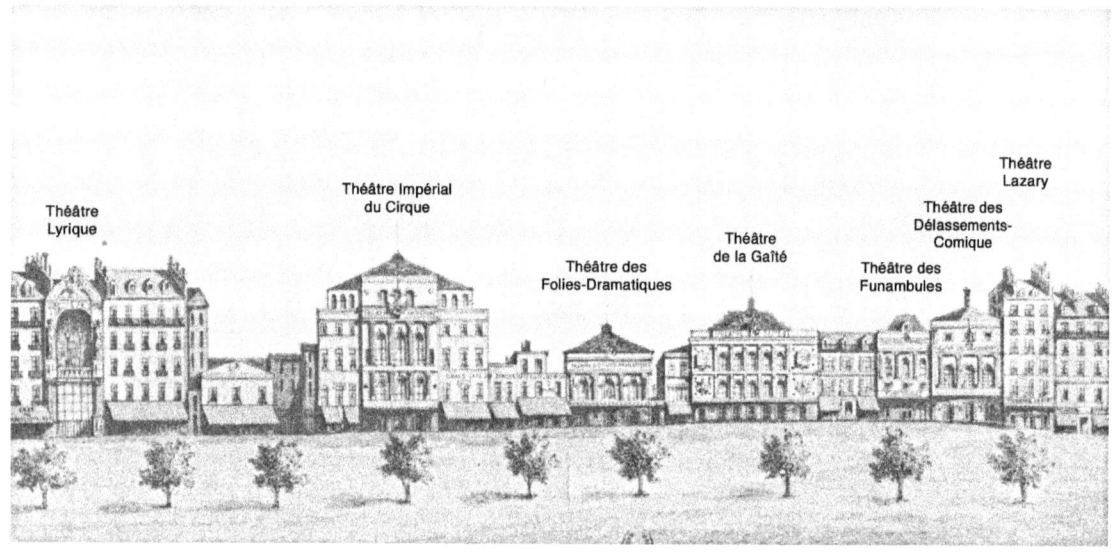

Theatres of the boulevard du Temple in Paris (Bibliothèque nationale de Paris)

It was clearly a substantial building, and what is interesting in the description is that it is described as being internally polygonal in appearance, following the contours of the circular arena. The building had been leased to them by Francois Delpont and on the expiry of the lease and the subsequent redevelopment of the area, the brothers were forced once again to move. This time they returned to the site of Astley's Amphitheatre, on the rue du Faubourg de Temple.

Here they carried out extensive refurbishments and the new (and second) Cirque Olympique was opened in February 1817. There were some innovative design ideas incorporated into the new building but its opulence knew no bounds.

La salle, de forme semi-circulaire, raccordée aux avant-scène par des tangents, a 21.50 mètres de largeur et 19.50 mètres de longeur, mesurée du fond des loges.

Le parterre est remplacé ici par l'arène pour l'exercise des cheveaux, est l'orchestre présente une nouveauté qui mérite d'être signalé. Jusqu'ici l'on n'avait pas trouvé le moyen de ménager un emplacement convenable pour l'orchestre, indispensable pour aux représentations théâtrales, et le public était fatigué de la vue des ouvriers apportant, morceaue par morceau, un orchestra improvisé, et du bruit que l'ajustement de ces pièces occasionnaient. L'architecte a ingénieusement paré à ces inconvénients. Aussitôt que les exercises équestres sont terminés, on vois se detachér le partie de la circonférence du cirque qui touche presque le théâtre, et s'avancer ver le milieue de la salle comme un tiroir du commode. Ce tiroire porte les pupitres, les tabourets, et les chaises destinés aux musiciens. L'orchestre arrive au lieue convenable, comme par enchantement, par un mécanisme trés simple qui est mis en movement au-dessous du théâtres, sans bruit et sans qu'on aperçoive presque aucun ouvrier.

Au rez-de-chaussée, on a pratiqué, autour de l'enceinte du manège et en arrière des banquettes de galerie, un rang de baignoires grillés, d'où l'on peut parfaitement voir l'équitation et le spectacle. Au-dessus, ce sont trois rangs de galeries et de stalles avec de vaste amphithéâtres dans les fonds.
La decoration de la salle représente l'intérieur d'une riche et vaste tent d'étoffe, brochée d'or et d'argent, comme on en voyait au temps de la chevalerie pour les fêtes et les tournois. Douze colonettes en fer forgé et d'un seule morceau, représentant des lances dorées, de 188 millimètres de diamètre et de 15.60 mètres de hauteur, supportent la coupole et les différent rangs des loges.

La devanture de la première galerie est ornée de bas-reliefs retraçant des jeux olympiques; celle de la seconde galerie représente des enfants conduisants des chevaux. Le restant de la salle est décoré en draperies de couleur chamois, rehaussées d'or et d'argent. Les lances dorée supportent, à leurs partier supérieures, des trophées militaire, formé des armes et des attrributs de toutres les nations et de tous les siècles, depuis le bonnet phrygien et le casque du soldat romain jusqu'au chapeau du tambour-major, le shako de voltigeur et le turban de mamaluk, depuis le casse-tête du sauvage jusqu'au sabre du grenadier.

Les chevaux entrent dans l'arène et en sortent par deux larges ouvertures practiquées dans le bas des avant-scènes, et fermées par des portiéres. L'ouverture de l'avant-scène et 11.70 mètres de large sur 9.75 mètres de hauteur. Le rideau représente des draperies de couleur chamois, rehaussées d'or et d'argent. Les draperies de haut sont en ponceau et or. La salle est parfaitement éclairée par un lustre qui l'emporte, par sa grandeur et par le nombre de ses becs, qui est de cent vingt, sur tous ceux qui existent aujourd'hui dans les théâtres de la capitale. La suspension de ce lustre est absolument indépendante des supports de la coupole, et ne peut pas conséquent, inspirer la moindre crainte. (Donnett 1921, cited Dupavillon 1921)

[The hall, semi-circular in shape, connected to the proscenium by tangents, is 21.50 metres wide and 19.50 metres long, measured from the back of the boxes.

The parterre is replaced here by the arena for the exercise of the horses, and the orchestra presents a novelty which deserves to be pointed out. Hitherto no means had been found of managing a suitable place for the orchestra, indispensable for theatrical performances, and the public was tired of the sight of the workmen bringing, piece by piece, an improvised orchestra, and the noise that the adjustment of these parts caused. The architect ingeniously avoided these drawbacks. As soon as the equestrian exercises are finished, one sees detaching the part of the circumference of the circus which almost touches the theatre, and advancing towards the middle of the room like a chest of drawers. This drawer carries the desks, stools, and chairs intended for the musicians. The orchestra arrives at the right place, as if by magic, by a very simple mechanism which is set in motion below the theatre, without noise and without almost any worker being seen.

On the ground floor, around the enclosure of the riding school and behind the benches in the gallery, there is a row of grilled tub seats, from which one can perfectly see the horse riding and the show. Above, there are three rows of galleries and stalls with the vast amphitheatres in the background.

The decoration of the room represents the interior of a rich and vast tent of cloth, brocaded with gold and silver, as one saw in the time of chivalry for festivals and tournaments. Twelve one-piece wrought iron colonettes, representing golden spears, 188 millimetres in diameter and 15.60 metres high, support the dome and the different rows of boxes.

The front of the first gallery is decorated with bas-reliefs depicting the Olympic Games; that of the second gallery represents children driving horses. The rest of the room is decorated in buff-coloured draperies, accented with gold and silver. The golden lances support, at their upper part, military trophies, made up of the arms and attributes of all nations and all centuries, from the Phrygian cap and the helmet of the Roman soldier to the hat of the drum major, then a voltigeur's shako and the mamaluk's turban, from the savage's club to the grenadier's sabre.

The horses enter the arena and leave it through two large openings at the bottom of the stages, and closed by doors. The opening of the front stage is 11.70 metres wide by 9.75 metres high. The curtain represents draperies of buff colour, enhanced with gold and silver. The upper draperies are in ponceau and gold. The room is perfectly lighted by a chandelier which exceeds it by its size and by the number of its burners, which is one hundred and twenty, out of all those which exist today in the theatres of the capital. The suspension of this chandelier is absolutely independent of the supports of the dome, and therefore cannot induce the slightest fear. *Author's translation*]

The Cirque Olympique continued on this site until March 1826, when, during a performance, the pyrotechnical effects caused a fire that quickly spread throughout the building and completely destroyed it. Undeterred, the two brothers set about creating a new Cirque, this time on the Boulevard du Temple. Built to the designs of the architect Alexandre Bourla, it became the third incarnation of the Cirque Olympique, under the ownership of Louis Dejean. It continued for some twenty years before it was remodelled and renamed the Théâtre du Cirque National, under the management of Hippolyte Hostein. In 1853 the name changed yet again to the Théâtre du Cirque Impèrial. The building was finally demolished in 1862, after which time Hostein moved his company to the newly built Théâtre Impèrial du Châtelet. For a brief time, this theatre became locally referred to as the Noveau Cirque Olympique but, sadly, the theatre became more used for dramas, operas, and vaudevilles rather than circus.

Louis Dejean obtained a licence in 1826 for a summer canvas circus on the Carré Marigny on the famous Parisian boulevard, the Champs Élysée. Here, the Franconis would present their summer performances. By 1838, Dejean had engaged one of the foremost architects of the time, Jacques Ignace Hittorf, to design a permanent circus building on the site.

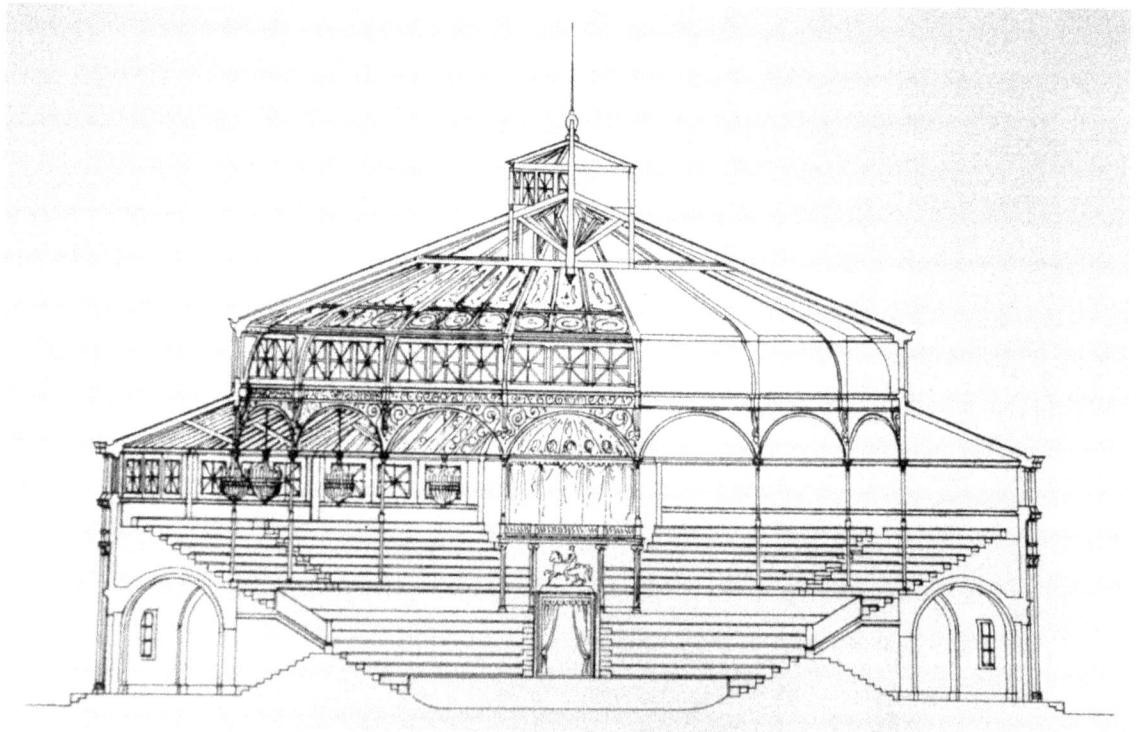

Plan of the Champs Élysée Cirque, Paris c.1840 (Bibliothèque nationale de Paris)

Hittorf was a German born architect who was responsible for the designs of many notable buildings and structures in Paris, including the Gare du Nord, and the Rotunda. When he died in 1867, his obituary specifically mentioned the circus building on the Champs Élysée. By the time of his death the circus had, as many did, undergone several name changes. In 1848 it had been the Cirque National de Paris and in 1853 the Cirque de l'Impératrice. It would later become known as the Cirque d'Été (the summer circus).

> The most important, however, of which is the Grand Cirque Olympique, now called of the Empress [Cirque de l'Impératrice], built in 1839. This is well known to all who have visited Paris as a sixteen-sided building, capable of holding 4,000 spectators, for equestrian exercises, above 134 ft. in diameter, and covered by a roof without a tie beam, the stability of which depends upon the circular or polygonal curb against which the feet of the rafters rest; attached is stabling for the horses of the troupe. The decorations are conceived in the best taste, so that the vastness of the area without any central pillars and the elegance of the ornamentation place it in the same rank with the large and more costly productions of the like nature of the times of the ancients. In 1851 a larger and more sumptuous circus was erected on the Boulevard des Filles du Calvaire in nine months, with increased reputation to the author, and enriched, as was also the other Circus, with the sculptures of the eminent Pradier and Duret, and the pictures of M. Berrias. (*The Building News* Vol. 14 May 10 1867)

The 1851 construction mentioned in the above obituary was the Cirque Napoleon, named in honour of Louis Napoleon Bonaparte the nephew of the Emperor Napoleon Bonaparte. Louis Dejean commissioned Hittorf to design and construct a winter home for his company. The Cirque d'Été was in operation from May through to October and a more permanent winter quarters was needed. The new circus opened its doors in December 1852.

As in the Cirque d'Été, no stage was included in the design so that the building would be used mainly for equestrian displays and other activities. The new circus was constructed as a twenty-sided polygon, 42 metres in diameter with a height of 27.5 metres to the top of the cupola surmounting the roof. There were no internal columns to support the dome. The weight of the cupola was supported by reinforced columns at the angle of each external wall. With no internal columns, a full view of the arena was enabled for all spectators. The internal decorations were opulent, especially the ceiling. This was modelled on a Roman design and this impressive feature can still be seen today, albeit slightly masked by a lighting rig that was installed later. The original seating existed mainly of narrow benches with hard back supports, covered in crimson material. There were three concentric seating areas, with a promenade running around the building behind the upper bank of seats. Boxes were not added until around 1923. The original capacity when opened was said to have been almost 4000 but now, with later modifications, it is only 1800. Externally the building was as ostentatious as it was inside. The façade displays a sculpted frieze depicting the creation of the horse by the god Neptune, and its subsequent training by the goddess Minerva. Two equestrian statues framed the entrance to the circus; one depicting an Amazon, the other a Greek warrior. Both the frieze and the statues can still be seen today. It is worthwhile mentioning at this point that the Cirque Napoleon presented the first ever demonstration of the 'flying' trapeze when, in 1859, Jules Léotard became the first aerial performer to fly from bar to bar. A memorial plaque to this historic event is still in place in the current building.

Plaque in memory of Jules Léotard at the Cirque d'Hiver, Paris (Courtesy of Caroline Palmer)

In 1872, Louis Dejean retired and the management of both of his circuses was taken on by Victor Franconi, youngest son of Antonio Franconi. With the deposition of Louis Napoleon Bonaparte (Napoleon III) in 1870 and the subsequent declaration of the second French Republic, it seemed somewhat incongruous that the Cirque should still bear the epithet of 'Napoleon'. So, in 1873, Franconi altered the name of the venue to its current name of the Cirque d'Hiver (winter circus). The building is still in operation today.

Cirque d'Hiver (Late C19th postcard courtesy of Gilles Maignant)

Franconi closed the Cirque d'Été in 1899 and later in 1907 leased the Cirque d'Hiver to a film producer, who turned the circus into a cinema. But fortunately for the circus a theatrical entrepreneur, Gaston Desprez, acquired the lease and began to return the building to its former glory. It was completely refurbished and modified and recommenced as a circus again in October 1923, under the artistic directorship of the famous Fratellini family. Desprez finally sold the Cirque d'Hiver to the four Bouglione brothers in 1924 and it is still the new generation of the Bouglione family that keeps the Cirque d'Hiver Bouglione as the longest running and most successful Cirque today. The Cirque has an extensive circus museum that is well worth visiting if you are ever lucky enough to be in Paris. A taste of what is on display can be seen briefly online[1]. Both the 1955 film *Trapeze* and the 2016 film *Chocolat* were filmed at the Cirque d'Hiver and give a visual idea of how the Cirque may have looked in different periods of its existence.

In competition with the Cirque d'Hiver was the nearby Cirque du Chateau d'Eau. In 1875, the American equestrian and circus entrepreneur Jim Myers took the lease for twenty years at a rate of £2560 per annum on the courtyard of a block of commercial buildings known as the Magasin Réunis. Here, with the assistance of English contractors Messrs. Defries, the courtyard was covered with a painted glazed roof and within the ensuing space a complete circus was constructed out of iron and masonry[2]. There was accommodation for 4000 seated spectators, with additional space in boxes, in the balcony, and standing. Stables were situated under the rising seats and could accommodate eighty horses, plus elephants, camels, and lions. The circus complex also contained a large saloon 250 feet in length, lined with looking glasses, red velvet hangings, and fountains. A 110-foot American Bar fronted the circus, next to the Place du Chateau d'Eau (now the Place de la République). Myers presented his Cirque Américain here, as well as touring around Europe, until 1882 when accrued debts forced him to put his outfit up for auction.

*Place de Chateau d'eau (*The Builder *18 December 1875)*

Another Parisian circus that also opened in 1875 was the Cirque Fernando. Ferdinand Beert was a Belgian equestrian and acrobat who had been employed at both of Dejean's circuses for several years. During this time, he took the stage name of Fernando. Around 1870 he decided to form his own circus and his initial performances were given under canvas in the Montmarte district. At the beginning of 1874, Fernando acquired the lease on a small plot of land on the corner of the Rue des Martyrs and he commissioned a local architect, Gridiane, to design his new circus. Set within its square plot, the amphitheatre was a sixteen-sided polygon with an internal diameter of 34 metres. The metallic framed roof was constructed in two concentric circles. The inner circle formed an elevated cupola supported by sixteen cast iron columns. The walls of the cupola, and the surmounting lantern, had windows to allow daylight in to the arena, so that natural light could be used for rehearsals and daytime performances. Evening performances could be lit by sixteen gas chandeliers suspended from the circumference of the cupola. There was seating for some 2000 spectators, arranged in thirteen steeply raked rows of padded benches, with a narrow promenade for standing clients situated behind the upper most row of benches. It was, compared with other

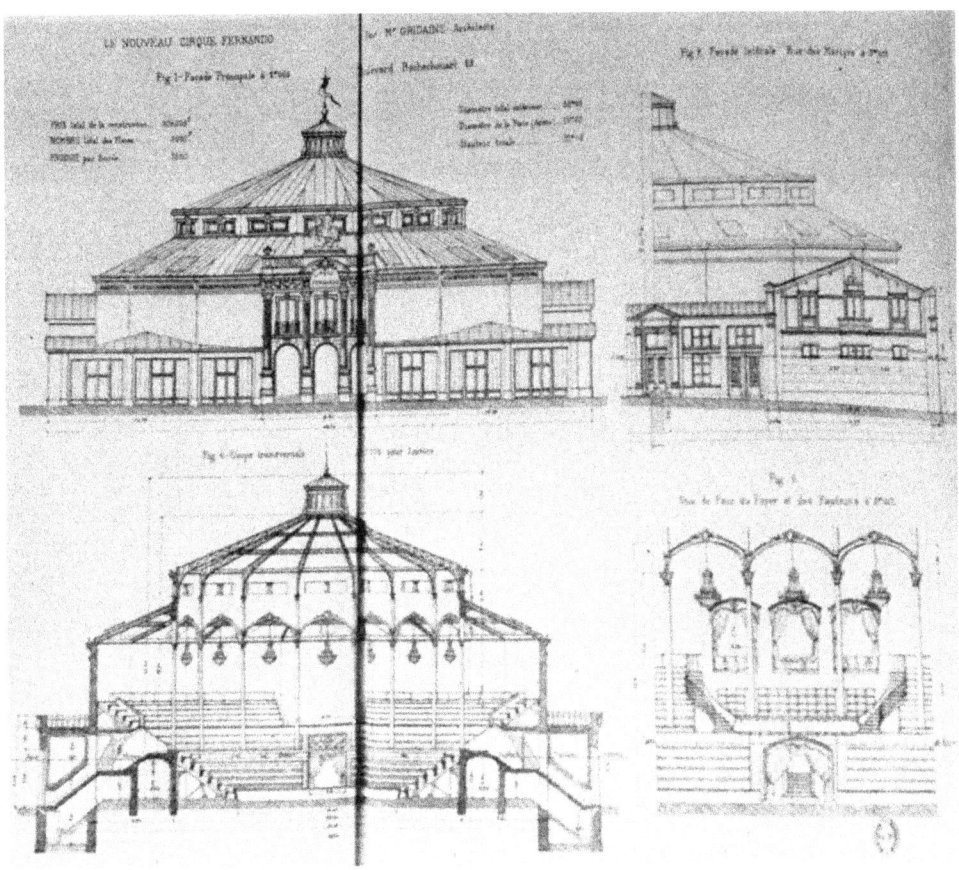

Plans for the Cirque Fernando (Bibliothèque nationale de Paris)

circuses in Paris, a relatively small venue but this did provide a feeling of intimacy that some of the others may have lacked.

The Cirque Fernando opened for business in June 1875 and became a regular attraction for artists and writers of the Bohemian area in which it was situated. Toulouse Lautrec was a regular visitor and was allowed to make many sketches of the artists in rehearsal. Similarly, Edgar Degas produced his famous sketch of the aerialist Miss La La (Olga Brown) while she was at the Cirque Fernando[3]. One of Fernando's chief attractions was a clown known as *Boum-Boum*. Born Geronimo Medrano in Spain in 1849 he became central to the Cirque Fernando's success, until he left the company in 1889. The Cirque Fernando, now under the management of Louis Fernando, entered into a very unsettled period culminating in the circus being put up for sale in 1897. Who should buy the circus but Geronimo 'Boum-Boum' Medrano? He promptly renamed the venue as the Cirque Medrano and it opened its doors in the December of that year. The Cirque Medrano continued in Paris for many years, right up until 1963, when its doors finally closed. But this was not the end of the circus building. The Bouglione brothers took over the building and renamed it the Cirque du Montmartre. In this guise the venue continued until January 1971. After a short period, demolition work was begun in January 1973, almost 100 years after it had first been built.

It was mentioned above that the clown Boum-Boum had left the Cirque Fernando in 1889 to join the company of the Nouveau Cirque. Joseph Oller, a Spanish born amusement entrepreneur, had a plan to utilise a building that could be a swimming pool in the summer months and a circus, the Nouveau Cirque, in the winter. He found such a building; the empty Panorama de Reischoffen on the rue saint Honoré, with a large rotunda that would be suitable for both of these ventures. To oversee the refurbishment of the project he engaged the architect Gridaine. The ground within the rotunda was excavated to a depth of 10 feet to accommodate a water reservoir for the swimming pool. The circus ring was fixed on a central metal plate that was mounted on a hydraulic pillar to allow it to be submerged. The ring floor was of slatted wood, enabling water to flow into the space created as it was lowered. The traditional sawdust flooring of the ring was replaced by a large removable carpet. Another technical innovation was that the entire building was lit by electricity, although gas was also installed as a back-up system. This was the first circus building to be lit by electricity in

France, although the first to be solely lit by electricity was the Leeds Hippodrome and Coliseum in England in 1885.

Cirque Medrano (Late C19th postcard courtesy of Gilles Maignant)

The venue opened on 12 February 1886 as the Arènes Nautique but the swimming pool aspect of the project was not as popular as Oller had anticipated. Soon the building became used solely for circus performances and known as the Nouveau Cirque, although water spectaculars and pantomimes became a regular feature of the Cirque. An annexe was also constructed to provide stabling for 20 horses, generators and other machinery, as well as for offices and dressing rooms. The traditional 13 metre diameter ring was surrounded by six raked rows of individual chairs with folding seats. Behind these seats was a circle of 56 boxes, each holding five persons. Beyond the boxes was a promenade for standing spectators. The actual seating capacity was only 870, although Oller boasted that the circus could hold 2000 people. In time, the promenade would be refurbished to allow for seated spectators. The decoration was in the Neo-Baroque style with 11 decorated frescoes of the Roman circus. The orchestra was situated high on a balcony over the ring entrance. Relatively small in comparison with some of the other Parisian circuses, the 33-metre diameter amphitheatre created a degree of intimacy, which was especially a great advantage to the clowns of the early company, including Boum-Boum and then Footit and Chocolat.

The Nouveau Cirque became a very popular venue for the well-heeled Parisians and continued under various managers until April 1926, when it finally closed its doors and was then demolished. In its place were built office buildings and it is now the site of the luxury Mandarin Oriental Hotel.

A rival to the Nouveau Cirque opened in January 1906. The Cirque Metropole was a large four storey high, brick-built construction with a glass dome supported by a metal frame. The amphitheatre was significantly larger than that of the Nouveau Cirque, with an internal diameter of 42 metres. It was reported that the Metropole could accommodate 6000 spectators. A ring of boxes surrounded the arena. Behind these was the large promenade, above which was a ring of arm chairs. Beyond these were two further balconies of seats. Stabling was in the basement. In 1907, the venue was renamed the Cirque de Paris and continued with a chequered career throughout its existence. Variously it was used as a venue for cinema, variety performances, sports events, and of course circus. The Cirque de Paris was eventually closed in 1930 and later demolished.

Although not strictly circuses, the Hippodromes of Paris have to be mentioned. During the latter half of the nineteenth century there were six Hippodromes constructed in the city[4], some of them overlapping in chronological use. These catered for thousands of spectators, who flocked to see equestrian spectacles, carriage races, processions, and tournaments. The Hippodromes also provided further venues for equestrian circus performers of the period, indeed the first, the Hippodrome de l'Étoile (1845 – 1856), was under the management of Victor Franconi. Boum Boum Medrano managed the Hippodrome du Champs de Mars (1885 – 1894) for a short period before establishing the Cirque Medrano.

If Paris was the European capital of circus during the nineteenth century, it is hardly surprising that many other major towns and cities around France soon also boasted permanent circus buildings. Most of these were constructed of stone and metal and followed the polygonal or circular models of those in Paris. Dupavillon (1982) mentions over 20 such buildings across France. One might expect a proximity to Paris, as the epicentre, but the sites range from Toulons in the south, Montluçon in the centre, Boulogne in the north, and many places in between.

If Britain had been the cradle of the circus, then France had seen its wider development. The circuses of Paris provided inspiration for other European cities to embrace circus and construct their own circus buildings.

Cirque Municipal, Douai (Early C20th postcard courtesy of Gilles Maignant)

Interior view of Troyes Cirque Municipal (Postcard, author's collection)

Notes

1. Our story|Cirque d'Hiver Bouglione (cirquedhiver.com)

2. *The Builder* 18 December 1875 Vol 33. P1131

3. A complete chapter is devoted to the life of Miss La La in; Ward. S, (2021) *Artistes of Colour; Ethnic Diversity and Representation in the Victorian Circus.* Modern Vaudeville Press

4. The horse and its heritage - Hippodromes for shows in Paris in the 19th century (culture.fr)

CHAPTER 7

CIRKUS TO ZIRKUS - FROM SCANDINAVIA TO AUSTRIA

Philip Astley is hailed as being the 'father of the modern circus' and many people believe, therefore, that he was the first performer of his kind. He may well have been the entrepreneur that brought the entertainment structure of circus together in a dedicated space, before a paying audience but he was certainly not the first performer. There were many equestrian performers, acrobats, jugglers contemporary with him and indeed before him. Antonio Franconi, for example, was a performer of note long before his association with Astley in Paris. Once the concept of circus had spread outwards from the United Kingdom into mainland Europe, and Astley had constructed his first amphitheatre in Paris, prominent performers and would be circus entrepreneurs in their own right began to see the merit of more permanent circus venues. Admittedly, many of the early amphitheatres were constructed from wood but, as the nineteenth century progressed more stone and brick-built circuses were erected. With Paris being the epicentre of the circus world by the mid-century there was a corresponding wave of prominent circus building across Europe. Circus seemed more fashionable and well supported on the Continent in comparison to Britain, something that the English clown, Charley Keith, alludes to in a letter published in *The Era* of 11 January 1863;

> Having been occupied in some of the first class equestrian establishments on the Continent, I have always found them to be the most fashionable resorts for all classes, and I am certain that were an equestrian circus of a superior description erected in London on the continental principle, with the stables thrown open as a promenade for the public to view the stud of horses (an indulgence the English have never been allowed to witness), that the circus would become the most fashionably attended place of amusement. In England it is considered a great honour to appear before the mayor of the town or some high personage, while on the Continent the nobility nightly patronise the circus as well as the humbler class, and it is a common occurrence to appear before royalty, a box being always fitted up for their reception ...

several other well-known Continental directors, would have speculated long ago in a London circus but the want of a suitable place to erect such a building was the cause of their not carrying out their intentions. Then why cannot a central piece of ground be bought, and plenty of gentlemen would be found ready to take the case in hand, and, no doubt, some of our spirited English circus managers would be first in the field, who would be certain to reap the reward of their liberality in erecting a first-class Cirque, and the thanks of the public for making equestrianism as fashionable and as popular as it is at present in Paris, Vienna, Berlin, Madrid, Lisbon, and other large cities on the Continent.

Charley Keith's first-hand experience of Continental circuses is illuminating because although circus was popular in Britain it would be several years before Hengler erected his stone-built circuses around the country, thereby emulating the developments in Paris. And clearly from Keith's text, the circus was well established across the continent by the date of his writing the letter in December of 1862. Although he lists some of the major European cities, by the latter part of the century there were circus buildings from the Scandinavian countries in the north right down to the Mediterranean countries in the south, and indeed beyond.

One of the most northerly circus buildings was constructed in Trondheim, Norway. In 1886, a disused brewery building was bought by developer Hans Oscar Kunig, the brother of the Norwegian architect Johan Kunig. The building was converted into a circus in 1887 and operated as such for ten years, until it was sold to the Salvation Army in 1897. By 1909 it had been sold again and became a cinema theatre. The newly formed Trondheim Student Community bought the building and it was used as a meeting place until 1929, when the Community commissioned a new building just across the bridge from the old Circus. What is interesting about this new building, constructed of red brick and named the Cassa Rossa, is that the design brief demanded that;

> The basic idea of the old hall [shall] be retained in the new one ... and as far as possible approach the circular basic form[1].

And indeed, this idea was carried through. A visit to the Student Community website[2] offers a video guide through the building, and the main hall, for all intents and purpose, could be a circus. Now the space is used for meetings, concerts, and other performances. The old Circus continued as a cinema after the students had left until World War 2, when the Germans occupied it and used it as a warehouse. After the war it fell into disuse and was eventually demolished in 1951 and the space became a car park. But its memory lingers on in the Cassa Rossa.

Circus building in Trondheim, Norway c.1918 (Courtesy of NTNU)

It would be a few years later that the capital city of Oslo (formerly known as Christiania until 1925) would have a circus building of its own. It was constructed of red brick and built in a Renaissance style, possibly inspired by the circus building in Copenhagen, Denmark[3]. Designed by Ove Ekman, it covered an area of 3200 square metres and was recorded as being 40 metres wide and 32 metres high, with an audience capacity of 2500. The audience sat in the amphitheatre and on a balcony. The circus also had a permanent royal box, reflecting the high status that circus had within society at that time. There were nine entrance and exit doors around the building, the largest and main entrance opening to the Tivoli side. The circus incorporated a small stage and there was stabling for up to 70 horses and other animals, the stables having a floor area of 600 square metres and being seven metres high. Beneath the stables were other store rooms and an ice room. Berthelsen (2007) informs us that connected to the amphitheatre was a square engine house that supplied hot steam for heating the building as well as an electric generator for the lighting. The building was constructed at the behest of Gotthold Schumann[4], founder of the Schumann dynasty of which we will discover more later in this work, and opened on March 15 1890. There was no resident Norwegian circus company at the time and the building continued to be used for visiting foreign circus companies and other entertainments such as cinema and concerts until October 16 1935, when the final performance was given by Circus Schumann. After this time the building was demolished and the area around it, known as Tivoli, was redeveloped into the City Hall.

Circus building in Oslo, Norway (Early C20th image courtesy of Oslo Museum)

Gotthold Schumann was also responsible for establishing the first circus building in Sweden in 1884, in Gothenburg, although there're had been temporary 'summer theatres' before this date in the Lorensberg Park. Schumann's building was in the park and became known as the Circus Lorensberg. It was a mixed material construction, with the stabling being built of stone but the actual amphitheatre was of wood. In 1898, Josef Möller's Cirkus du Nord was performing in the building when the following incident occurred that made the international press;

A fatal accident has happened to Signor Corradini, the director of the 'Cirque du Nord', Gothenburg. The great feat of this circus rider has attracted much attention. The performer rides his horse Good Boy on to a platform, which just gives foothold, and the whole is slowly hoisted to the roof of the building. When there Signor Corradini puts a match to various fireworks that surround the platform, and he and his horse are seen by the audience suspended from the roof. The horse had been noticed for two nights past to be somewhat restless owing to a new kind of firework having been used, and he reared and slipped off the platform, and along with his rider fell heavily to the ground. A strong wire, which was designed as a safeguard in case of such an accident and which (fastened to the saddle) was intended to hold horse and rider suspended, snapped with the weight. The horse was killed instantaneously and Corradini expired the following morning. (*Leominster News and Northwest Herefordshire & Radnorshire Advertiser* 6 May 1898)

Being constructed largely of wood, the building was always susceptible to fire and, in January 1900, just such a thing happened while Cirkus Bergman was in residence. The building was very quickly rebuilt, again of wood, and opened just 26 days later with a performance by Circus Wulff. To minimise the risk of fires the amphitheatre had an

Lorensberg Circus, Sweden c. 1963 (Courtesy of Lennart Strandner)

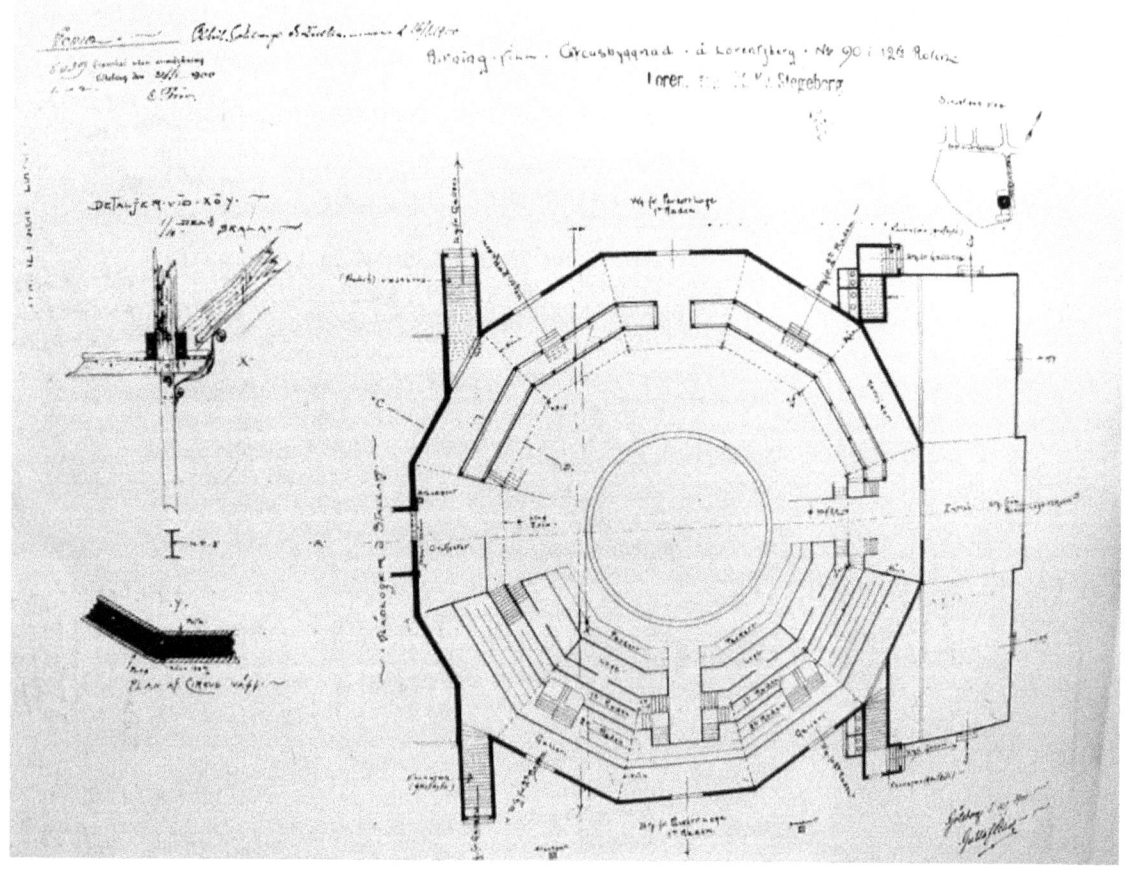

Lorensberg Circus ground plan c.1900 (Courtesy of Lennart Strandner)

internal iron construction and bricks were used in part. The best seats in the house, which were in the boxes, were covered in red cloth. The rest of the seating was painted in yellow with black decoration. The outside of the circus was painted green. The amphitheatre became used for other entertainments such as sporting events, theatre, and music events. It was eventually demolished in 1969 and the space is now a parking area, although plans are being put in place for a redevelopment of the area to be known as *Cirkusplatsen* which will include commercial property and residential homes.

One might have expected that the capital city of Stockholm would have been the first to boast a circus building, but it was not until around 1868 that the first building appeared. Before that date, Didier Gautier had a menagerie and some other open air 'circus style' entertainments in Stockholm's Djurgården. The Djurgården is a small island in central Stockholm that is now famous for its museums, galleries, and amusements. It also has a network of paths that run across the island and is a popular attraction for residents and tourists alike. Historically, it began in the sixteenth century as a game park but by the eighteenth century it had become more of a recreational area. Gautier sold his menagerie and 'circus' in 1868 to Adèle Houcke, the widow of the circus owner Jean Lèonard Houcke. She founded the Circus Lèonard with her sons, Adolphe, Jules, and Theodore and commissioned the first circus building in the park. Like others of the period, it was built of wood and, like many others, was destroyed by fire at the end of the 1880s. It was rebuilt in stone in 1892 and the building still stands today, very much as it was but now it is used for a variety of entertainment events.

Djurgården Circus, Stockholm, Sweden (Early C20th postcard, author's collection)

Almost 400 miles south-west of Stockholm, and situated at the eastern end of the Öresund Bridge that connects Sweden with Denmark, lies the port city of Malmö. Here, in January 1899, the Malmö Hippodrome was inaugurated. Circus Tanti was the first company to perform there. Although built initially for circus and other equestrian entertainments the Hippodrome became used as a venue for other entertainments and sporting events. The last real circus show performed there in 1922. After that the building was converted in to a theatre by Oscar Winge. In 1950 the building was sold to a Pentecostal church and continued as such until 1992, when it was bought by the city and renovated as a theatre once more. In 2008 it became the Stadstheater Malmö.

The building has seen much renovation and alteration over the years but the arched entrance, with reliefs of a lion and a horse, can still be seen today and the interior, although now a modern theatre, still reflects the original purpose.

The red brick building on Platensgaten in Linköping, a city some 125 miles south-west of Stockholm, was once a circus building. Opened in September 1912, it replaced two earlier and smaller wooden circus buildings in the city. Circus Orlando gave the opening performance. The circus had been founded by Henning Orlando in 1902 after he had bought the Circus Madigan. The rectilinear building had a vast glass dome to allow light into the arena. A circus café was also installed at the time, and it is still there today. By 1927, the original interior was stripped out and a new intermediate floor installed with a new auditorium where, like other circus buildings in the country, other entertainments could be presented. The ground floor became a garage. In 1959, the building was no longer used as a place of entertainment and became a car display room. Fortunately, in the 1980s the building was renovated once again as offices but the designers agreed to keep the exterior of the building much as it was originally. Internally it has been much altered but the company that owns the offices has acknowledged the history of the building with photos and a heritage display.

It is worth mentioning the Furuvikspark at this point. The park is near the town of Gävle, on the eastern Baltic coast of Sweden. It does have, as its website proclaims, 'one of the largest wooden circus arenas in Europe, the only permanent circus in Sweden with a live stage'[5]. The park was founded in 1900 as a zoo but it was not until 1938 that an open-air circus was created there when the park was bought by Gösta Nygren. A wooden circus building was then constructed in 1940 and became a venue for visiting circuses, as well as the summer performance space for the *Furuviksbarnen*, a children's circus. It was renovated in 1985 and then destroyed by fire in 1994. Subsequently rebuilt, it became a multi-arts venue rather than a circus. Furuvikspark itself is now an amusement park with a zoo and various rides. The old wooden circus building still stands, much renovated, but it now largely used by park employees and for staff training.

Across the Öresund Bridge from Malmö in Sweden is Copenhagen, the capital city of Denmark. On 8 May 1886 a newly built Circus building (the Cirkusbygningen in Danish) was inaugurated by the circus impresario Ernst Renz. This was not the first 'permanent' circus to be constructed in Denmark as a circus owner named Pertolleti built a wooden amphitheatre in the town of Nørrebro in 1830. It could seat 1800 people. Although intended as being a permanent structure it was destroyed by fire in 1833 and never rebuilt. By 1886, Renz had been responsible for erecting elegant circus buildings in several cities across Europe, as we shall discover. The new Circus was built to a design by the architect H. Brinkopff. It was circular in construction and could accommodate 1800 people. Attached stabling could hold up to 100 horses. The interior decorations were elaborate with paintings on the ceiling and walls of acrobats. Sculpted images of antique races on a frieze runs around the exterior of the building. In 1887, Renz sublet the building to Albert Schumann, the son of Gotthold Schumann. The circus subsequently hosted many of the famous circus names of the period; Busch, Orlando, Beketow, and Ciniselli. In 1914, tragedy struck when the building was consumed by fire. Only the outer walls, façade, and frieze were saved. The circus was rebuilt, with concrete roof and interior walls. It reopened its doors to the public in 1915 when the German circus of Sarrasani took the lease.

Circus building, Copenhagen, Denmark (Late C19th postcard, author's collection)

The Schumann brothers, Willy, Ernst, and Oscar nephews of Albert Schumann, took over the lease in 1918 and remained there until 1968, with a four-year break during World War 2. By the 1950s the circus was being run by the sons of Oscar Schumann. During this lengthy time the circus building became known as Circus Schumann. During the winter months the circus was not allowed to operate by the ruling of the city authorities and at these times the building was used as a cinema. In 1963, there were plans to change the building into a department store but after protests, and with a lack of the necessary funding for the project, the plans were dropped. The Benneweiss family then took over the lease in 1970 and continued performing during the summer months until 1990. During this period of its history the building was known as Circus Benneweiss. Since 1990, the circus building has been used for a variety of entertainments and Circus Roncalli gave the last full circus show there in 2003. Now the building is used as a 'dinner-show' venue that does include elements of acrobatic circus in its entertainment. The building is now a protected landmark and, externally, still exists very much as it did in its original days.

We cannot leave Scandinavia without a brief look at Finland. Although the country has a thriving circus scene with over twenty contemporary circus groups[6], historically circus did not have the impact there as in other European countries. However, in 1910 the Helsinki Hippodrome was opened. The building could seat 1000 people and had stabling for around 40 horses, so it was not large in comparison with some of the other circuses of the period. As well as hosting circuses it was also a venue for sports events, notably wrestling. It was demolished in 1950 and replaced by a sports hall that hosted some of the events in the 1952 Olympic Games. Now it is a training base for the Torpan Pojat professional basketball team.

Of the three Baltic states, it is only Latvia that has an historic permanent circus building. Albert Salamonsky, a Prussian, commissioned the building in the capital city of Riga in 1888. By this time, he had already founded circuses in Moscow and Berlin. In Riga the circus was known as Salamonsky Circus.

The architect of the original building is Janis Fridrihs Baumanis (Jānis Frīdrihs Baumanis, 1834-1891), the very first educated Latvian architect. The building at the time consisted of circus arena with spectacular cupola and two wings facing present-day Merķeļa Street. Initially, the main circus façade towards Merķeļa Street was built in classicism manner - highly popular style at the time. The building is also known for its extraordinary construction techniques. The structure of circus arena/cupola is made from railroad rails and its faceted dome is constructed from 16 meridian ribs joined by three main circles, which are located in the ribs' fractures and visually divide the cupola into three 'belts'. The main composition of the building - the ring - is 13m in its diameter, and circus arena could accommodate up to 1,700 visitors at its earliest construction. (Ostanevics, 2017:22)

The dome of the new circus building was distinctive and innovative in design. Epnere (2021 :43) compares the spatiality of the circus with the Byzantium Gregorian Church, centred on the circle and dome. The dome of the Salamonsky Circus was 76 feet in diameter and;

> The circus was illuminated by splendid, glass-encased gas lanterns; viewing was easy because of the rows of seats that gradually rose upwards. The circus was mindful of hierarchy; the management box, with seating also got journalists, was separated and elevated. Closer to the dome was a balcony and gallery with standing toom, for which the tickets were the cheapest. The orchestra was seated above the entrance to the arena. The building, with wood panelling and wooden seats, provided excellent acoustics; one could hear every whisper, let alone the loud rumbling of the drums, drawing he audience's attention to risky moments in the acts.

The arena could also be used for water spectaculars and in 1898 the first 'water pantomime' was presented at the Salamonsky Circus. The building was altered over the subsequent years. Stables were built at the rear of the building to accommodate both horses and elephants. The arena was reconfigured with a balcony and gallery added. This increased the audience capacity. At the front of the building an iron staircase was constructed that led to the upper level and an iron canopy was placed over the main entrance.

Sadly, by 1917 the effects of the war were being felt. The stables were used to house and sell horses deemed unfit for war work and by the end of the war the circus was in a sorry condition. Further renovations and refurbishments were carried out during the Soviet

Riga Circus, Latvia, c.1911 (Postcard courtesy of Lolita Lipinska)

Interior of the closed Riga Circus (Public domain image)

era, and the final round carried out in the 1960s led to what could be seen up until 2016, when it was closed for two years for external structural work to the façade. The building is now undergoing major renovation and reconstruction work to develop a new circus arena and a multi-arts complex.

In an online interview the director of Circus Riga, Māra Pāvula explained[7];

> At the moment, the historical building of Rīgas cirks is undergoing its first phase of reconstruction in the frame of ERAF project of improving energy efficiency. The work started last May and will finish this autumn. It means that in autumn we are returning to a renovated arena with a new innovative dome construction made out of CLT panels. As far as we know, it will be a unique solution for dome construction throughout the world. It will be a multifunctional open space with possibilities to organise standing events and to host circus performances in the arena and on the frontal stage. The next stages will be the construction of a black box theatre, the circus school, and residency apartments. The exact dates for the next phase are not yet clear. Architects are working with great respect to the architectural heritage, and have kept the original rail structure. The interior will be decorated with original wooden planks from the nineteenth century. We hope to organise the grand opening festival in the beginning of 2023.

Plans and diagrams of the proposed new venture can be viewed online[8], although recently received photographs[9] show that those proposed plans have yet to be achieved.

Ernst Renz, the founder of the Copenhagen circus, was a well-established figure in the circus world. By 1846 he had his own circus company in Berlin and was housed in a wooden circus building, until it was destroyed by fire in 1853;

> Renz's circus for equestrian performances had just caught fire, and the well-appointed fire brigade in full gallop on all sides towards the spot, where the vast wooden circular building, 80 feet in diameter and about 60 feet high, was, after the lapse of about ten minutes from it catching fire, one compact flame. The horses and wardrobe were saved ... The whole building

was burned down in comparatively a few minutes, at noonday, in bright sunshine, and a faulty supply of water. (*Evening Mail* 2 December 1853)

Renz then went on to construct another circus building on Georgenstrasse/ Friedrichstrasse but the land on which this was built was requisitioned in 1872 by the Berlin Metropolitan Railway. A new circus was commissioned on a site in Lindenstrasse and plans were described, as here in *The Builder* of 15 July 1876 [10];

> The front part of the ground, as far as it borders the street, is to serve for the erection of a residence for Herr Renz. The circus and the stables are to occupy the rear of the plot, the area of which is nearly two and a half acres. The circus is calculated to hold 4500 spectators, room being found for that number in an amphitheatre and two galleries. There is, besides, a row of private boxes, with a number of retiring rooms. The building also contains a stage for the orchestra; an arena, of a diameter of 43 feet; a stage of 5382 square feet, which may be thrown into one with the arena; all the necessary machinery for the transformation of the stage; a spacious principal vestibule, two side entrances, pay-offices, refreshment-rooms, riding corridor, saddling place, harness-room, room for dancing and gymnastic exercise, painters' room, and a few property rooms. Outside of the circus building proper there will be stables for 110 horses, with different connecting passages, stables for sick horses, and conveniences for the public, the artistes, and attendants. The whole building, with a façade rich in sculpture (the subject of our illustration) stands free. Carriage approaches are not provided but there is a wide glass-covered passage from the front part of the building to the road.

Sadly, these plans never came to fruition, as the illustration of the proposed circus shows what an elegant building this would have been. However, having received substantial compensation for the circus he had to give up in 1872, he was able to buy the Markthallenzirkus (literal translation Market Hall Circus). The building had been opened as a market hall in 1867 but had not been a commercial success. Its impressive size, 84 metres by 62 metres with a height of 15.5 metres made it far too large for its intended purpose. By 1873 it had been converted into a circus that could accommodate 4000 people. Albert Salamonsky took the lease and operated there until Renz bought a sixth month lease on the building in 1876. This then became the centre of Renz's

*Circus Renz, Berlin, Germany (*The Builder *15 July 1876)*

circus empire. Renz then bought the circus in 1886 and the building was redeveloped to accommodate 5000 spectators. It opened to the public in October 1889. When Ernst Renz died in 1892, the company was taken over by his son Franz but because of growing financial difficulties the Renz Circus was closed in the July of 1897. In 1899, Albert Schumann took over the building and operated Circus Schumann at this venue until 1918. After this time, it was used for mainly theatre performances, revue shows, and variety entertainments. The building was destroyed in the bombing of 1941. The street name in that area is still known as 'Am Zirkus' (at the Circus).

The Renz empire in Germany also included circus buildings in Hamburg and Breslau (later to be known as Wroclaw when it came to be a part of Poland). But Renz had competition. The Schumann family was developing its own circus empire and when the Circus Renz closed in Berlin in 1879, it was Albert Schumann who took over the building and who would eventually buy it. It then became known as Circus Albert Schumann. Schumann also built another permanent circus in a town named Löbtau, near Dresden, in 1898. Little is known about this building as it was destroyed, along with all documents in the bombing of World War 2.

Circus Busch was another company on the rise as Renz went in to decline. Paul Busch had established Circus Busch in 1884 in Svendborg, Denmark. By 1891 he had built a permanent circus in Hamburg and in 1895 he opened a 3500-seat circus in Berlin that included the facility to present water spectaculars.

Circus Busch, Berlin, Germany (Early C20th postcard, author's collection)

As with Hengler in Britain, water spectaculars were popular in European circuses. Much of the entertainment included boats of various description, swimming and diving, and general aquatic clowning. The *Northampton Mercury* of 27 February 1891 gives us an impression;

> In about a minute the arena is flooded with 25,000 gallons [approximately 95,000 litres] of warm water, upon which soon appear boats, canoes, ducks etc. The visitors [performers] arrive, a little regatta follows, several of the characters are pushed in the water, there are gallant rescues, and fun in endless variety.

Circus Busch remained in use until 1937, when it was demolished by the Nazis. By 1902 he was so successful that he was able to buy the old Renz building in Hamburg and in the following year the Breslau building. From a 1939 postcard it can be seen as a rectilinear building that fronts a polyhedral amphitheatre adorned with a lantern. The Breslau building continued in use until 1945.

Circus Busch, Breslau, Poland,1939 (Postcard, author's collection)

Although Renz, Schumann, and Busch appear to dominate the circus world in Germany there were two other companies who were responsible for circus buildings. The Blumenfeld brothers acquired a stone-built circus in 1914 in the town of Magdeburg. It had been originally constructed in 1896 but had frequently been used as a cinema. World War 1 put an end to most circus performances in the venue and in the post war era it was used mainly as a cinema and variety venue, with only the occasional circus performance. The building was badly damaged during bombing in 1945 and never rebuilt.

Hans Stosch-Sarrasani founded the Sarrasani Circus in 1902 near Dresden and he commissioned a permanent circus to be built in the city in 1912.

The (then) modern building was very tall, 36 metres in height, with a cupola 46.5 metres in diameter. The standard 13.5 metre circus ring had the facility to be lowered and flooded with water for water spectaculars. The arena was complete with a fully equipped stage and orchestra pit, and could seat almost 4000 spectators. The building

Circus Sarrasani, Dresden, Germany (Postcard, public domain image)

included a restaurant and an 'American Bar'; an American Bar being a 'long bar' arrangement as opposed to the more intimate tavern style bar. Behind the circus was stabling for up to 130 horses and space to accommodate a menagerie. The building survived successfully until the bombing of Dresden in 1945, when it was completely destroyed. The circus survived but Sarrasani, having problems with Hitler's regime, decided to move to South America in 1934. Hans Stolsch-Sarrasani died there shortly afterwards and the circus was continued by his son. The Sarrasani Circus became popular in Argentina and in the 1940s was proclaimed the 'Argentine National Circus' by Eva Peron.

Circus Krone, as a company, has a long history dating back to the 1860s when Karl Krone developed a travelling menagerie. But it was his son, Carl Krone, who brought the family name to recognition. Throughout the latter part of the nineteenth century and into the twentieth century Carl Krone travelled throughout Europe with his Circus-Menagerie, until in 1914 the name Circus Krone was officially adopted. By 1919 Krone had settled in Munich and commissioned a large wooden circus building that could accommodate 4000 spectators. It became known as the Kronebau and was used by Circus Krone during the winter months; the summer months were spent touring and the building was rented out for other purposes.

The Kronebau was destroyed in December 1944 by bombing and one year later a temporary wooden building was constructed on the site. This was relatively small and could only accommodate 1800 people. Circus Krone continued touring throughout Europe, using the temporary structure only during the winter months. It was in 1962 that a new building was constructed. This was constructed of reinforced concrete and faced with brick. It has a wooden cupola of 45 metre diameter, based on the design of the Cirque Napoleon in Paris. The new circus could accommodate 2800 spectators. The Kronebau is still in operation today from December through to March, with a monthly change on international circus programmes and can now accommodate 3000 seated spectators.

The Netherlands and Belgium also had significant circus buildings worth mentioning. Oscar Carré, a member of a German circus family, commissioned a stone-built circus to be constructed in the capital city of the Netherlands, Amsterdam. It opened in December 1887 and became the winter home of Circus Carré for many years. During the summer months, as with many other circus groups, Carré toured widely around Europe. After his death in 1911, the circus went bankrupt and it was turned into a variety theatre. The ensuing years showed a mixed success for the building and in 1968 it was proposed to demolish the building and construct a hotel on the site. The Amsterdam city council stepped in and deemed the circus as an historic building, thereby saving it from demolition. In 1977 it became the official theatre of Amsterdam and it was given the appellation of 'Royal'. Today, it is still in use as the Royal Carré Theatre.

Some of the original decorations to the façade of the building can still be seen and, although it has been internally renovated it still has much of the atmosphere that it

would have had in its original days. Each winter the Royal Carré Theatre presents *The World Christmas Circus* and the theatre reverts to its original intention. Elsewhere in the Netherlands, Carré visited the resort town of Scheveningen and wanted to construct a stone-built circus for his sole use. The city council refused and Carré left Scheveningen. It was Carré's rival, Albert Schumann, who prompted the authorities to build a permanent circus for the city, with himself as a consultant. It opened on 16 July 1904 and Schumann would continue to perform there until the outbreak of

Circus Carré, Amsterdam, Netherlands (C20th postcard, author's collection)

World War 1, when he moved his company to Denmark. The architect of the project, W. Liefland, constructed a 45-metre self-supporting dome over the building, inspired by the work of Eiffel. Many of the major circus companies of the period visited Schveningen but it was the Circus Strassburger who became famous there for its summer shows. By the 1960s the building was being threatened with demolition but due to a fire at the major theatre in the Hague, the Scheveningen building was acquired and totally refurbished as a new theatre. Almost all of the internal structure and decoration of the original circus was removed and it became a venue for many different performances. There was an attempt to bring the circus back to the building in the 1980s but this was short lived. Although the building still exists, no circus has performed there since that time. Now the AFAS Circustheater is a venue for musical theatre and concerts.

The building of the Nieuw (New) Circus in the Belgian city of Ghent still stands today. It was constructed in 1894 for the Equestrian Club of Ghent and designed by Emile De Weerdt. After a disastrous fire in 1920 only the external façade of the building remained. It was rebuilt in 1923 and could provide accommodation for 3500 spectators. Like many circus buildings of the period, it was used for other performances as well as for circus. The Nieuw Circus closed its doors in 1944 and then became a motor garage in 1947. In 1978 it was used to house a collection of vintage cars. It then became empty for some time but there are currently plans to convert the building into a dance club, along with office spaces, a restaurant, and a café.

In the capital city of Brussels, the Cirque Royale, as a performance venue, still survives after almost 150 years. It was opened in 1878 with a performance by Circus Renz. Appearing to be circular in shape, the building is a regular polygon. Twenty columns support the roof and the amphitheatre was originally decorated in an oriental style. Equestrian performances and water spectaculars were the popular styles of performance in its early days but pantomimes and ballets were also performed. From the early 1920s more variety theatre performances were given. The Cirque Royale is now a major venue for all different forms of entertainment and having undergone recent refurbishment can now seat 3500 spectators.

We have already mentioned the names Renz, Schumann, and Busch and it was these that were influential in the later circus buildings in Vienna, the capital of Austria. But it was a Latvian equestrian by the name of Christoph de Bach who was responsible for building the Circus Gymnasticus, which opened in June 1808. Bach had been a regular visitor to Vienna since 1802 and his equestrian shows were very popular. The building, on the popular place for recreation known as the Prater, was a sixteen-sided polygon constructed in stone around a wooden frame. The roof was supported by two circles of fourteen columns and the cupola was set with windows to allow light into the arena. The circus was complete with an imperial box as well as 18 private boxes. In total, the building could accommodate 3000 spectators. When de Bach died in 1834, the management of the circus passed on to his widow who continued the circus until 1852. By that time the building had become neglected and was subsequently sold and demolished.

In 1853, the same year that his circus in Berlin was destroyed by fire, Ernst Renz commissioned a new circus building on Grossen Fuhrmangasse (later to be renamed the Zirkusgasse in 1862) in Vienna. This was completed by 1854 and opened on 18 February 1854 and was known as the Renzbau. It had a twelve-sided floor plan with a diameter of 40 metres, and could seat 3559 people. A disastrous fire in the Ring Theatre in 1881, which claimed many lives, brought in new fire regulations, and the Renzbau was reconstructed in light of these in 1883, opening on 26 January 1884. When Ernst Renz died in 1892, his circus empire was taken over by his son Franz, including the Renzbau in Vienna. Bad management led to the decline of the Renz circus and the company went into liquidation in 1897. The building survived until

Interior view of the Circus Gymnasticus, Vienna, Austria c.1812 (Public domain image)

1930, when it burned down. It was then rebuilt as a variety theatre but was extensively damaged in the bombing of 1944. It was eventually demolished in 1957.

In the latter days of the Renzbau, various branches of the Schumann circus gave performances in the building. In 1892, Albert Schumann erected a wooden circus on Märzstrasse, opening on 20 April 1892. This was complete with electric lighting, and had direct connections from the stables into the arena. Its audience capacity was 3500. By 1903 this was redeveloped into a stone-built structure, opening the following year. It was circular in design and had a 50-metre diameter and was 22.5 metres to the top of the cupola. It had three spectator galleries and could accommodate 3200 people. The building survived until 1923 and the retirement of Schumann, after which time a school was built on the site.

In the same year as Albert Schumann built his wooden circus on Märzstrasse, Paul Busch opened a circus at the entrance to the Prater on 30 May 1892. The building, originally constructed in 1882, had been a circular Panorama so easily lent itself to be converted into a circus. The building had a seating capacity of 2600. It was 39 metres in diameter and 15 metres in height. Detailed plans have been digitised and are available on the Vienna Archive website[11]. Using it as his winter quarters, Busch rented out

Circus Schumann, Vienna, Austria (C20th postcard, author's collection)

the circus when he was not in residence to visiting companies such as Sarrasani, Max Schumann, and Krone. Like many circus buildings it underwent a later conversion, in this case into a cinema in 1920. It was known as the Circus Busch Cinema. No further circus performances were given in the building after this date. During the bombing of the city in World War 2 the building was extensively damaged and was demolished in 1945.

Circus buildings were not exclusive to northern Europe. South, beyond the Pyrenees and the Alps, circus buildings were also in evidence.

Interior view of Circus Renz, Vienna, Austria (Public domain image)

Notes

1. Samfundets Historie - Samfundet.no

2. Admission at Samfundet - Samfundet.no

3. Hilde Aase. Librarian at the National Library of Norway. Personal email to author, 1 September 2022

4. There were several branches of Circus Schumann appearing around Europe at this time, operated by Gotthold Schumann's sons. We know that it was the circus of Gotthold Schumann that appeared in Oslo (Christiania) in 1890 as there is an advertisement in *The Era* 17 May 1890 seeking performers for his circus there.

5. Furuviksparken | Visit Gävle (visitgavle.se)

6. Makela. J., *Experience Circus from Finland*. 24 April 2017. www.circustalk.com

7. *A powerhouse of contemporary circus in the Baltics – An interview with Riga Circus' Māra Pāvula*. Online at; A powerhouse of contemporary circus in the Baltics – An interview with Riga Circus' Māra Pāvula • Sirkuksen Tiedotuskeskus (sirkusinfo.fi)

8. *RIGA-CIRCUS - Manuelle Gautrand* (manuelle-gautrand.com)

9. Lolita Lipinska. Personal email to author, September 2022

10. *The Builder* Vol 34. P691 15 July 1876

11. Vienna Archive Information System. WAIS - Vienna Archive Information System - Tectonics (wien.gv.at)

CHAPTER 8

CIRCO TO CYRK - THE MEDITERRANEAN AND CENTRAL EUROPE

In southern Mediterranean Italy the circus had a long tradition. While we may associate Italy with the historic Roman structures such as the Circus Maximus and others of a similar design, these are related to the 'modern' circus in name only. The spectacles presented in these arenas were a far cry from the artistry of the circus we understand today. Charles Hughes, rival to Philip Astley, certainly brought the concept of circus to Italy in the eighteenth century;

> L'enorme successo crea subito moltissimi emuli, come Charles Hughes, le cui tournèe anche in Italia sono documentate sin da prima del 1770, che sarà per altro il primo ad utilazzare il temine circus dai dell'antica Roma tempi. (Giarola & Serena n.d.)

> [The enormous success [of Astley's circus] immediately created many imitators, such as Charles Hughes, whose tours in Italy are documented since before 1770, and who was the first to use the term circus [in Italy] since ancient Roman times. *Author's translation*]

Performers such as the Zoppè and Casartelli families can trace their history back to the beginning of the nineteenth century. However, the circus tradition within Italy was one of a travelling nature rather than in permanent buildings, many circuses performing in one ring tented structures. Other European circus groups also toured throughout Italy at this period but they mainly performed under canvas or in buildings constructed of wood. Eduard Wulff visited the exhibition in Torino (Turin) in 1884 and built such a structure on a grand scale.

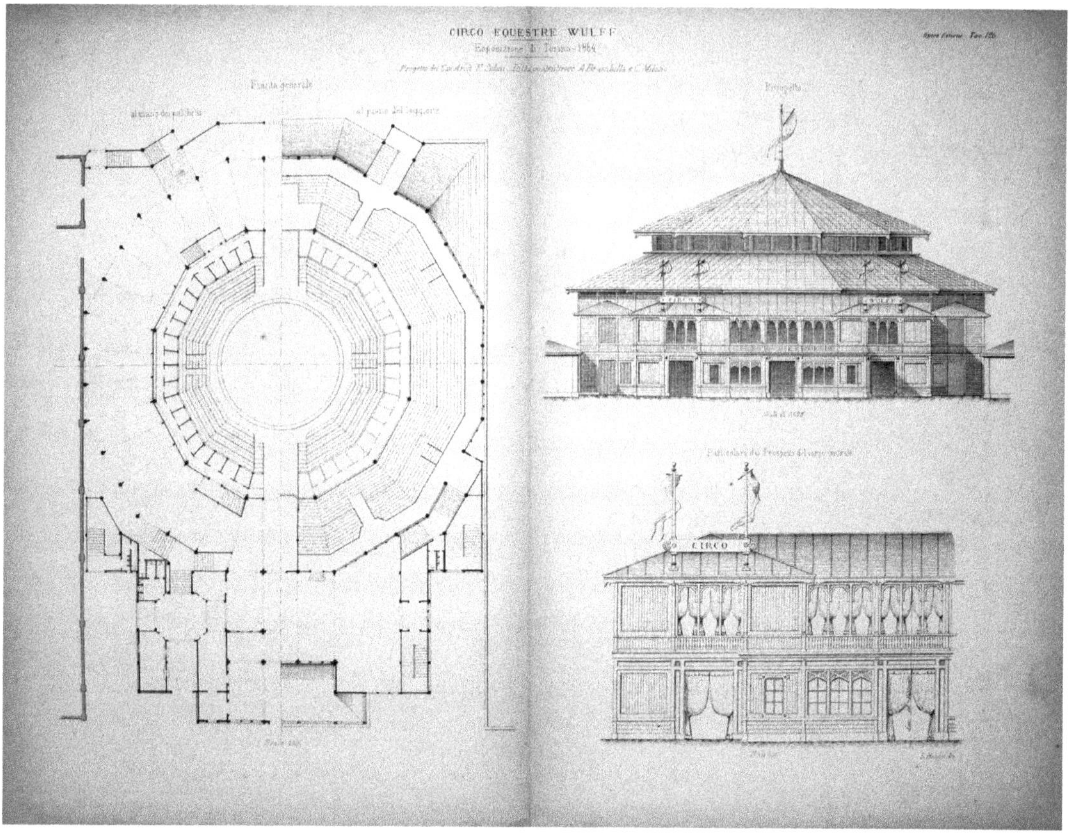

Plans for the Ecuestre Eduard Wulff in Torino, Italy, 1884 (Library of Congress)

Teatro Politeama in Palermo, Sicily (Public domain image)

It is also the fact that in many towns around the country there were theatre buildings which were used on occasions for visiting acrobatic and equestrian performances. In the city of Catania on the island of Sicily, Pappalardo (2013/2014) lists twelve different theatres, some of them dating to the early nineteenth century, in which equestrian and acrobatic performances were given spanning the dates 1839 to 1885. Some of these buildings are still in existence and in Palermo, the capital city of Sicily, the Teatro Politeama Garibaldi, is a fine example of such a theatre still used today.

Across Italy there were many such theatres as the ones on Sicily; in Verona, Cremona, Vercelli, Parma, and Verme to name but a few. These are explored in full in works by Sgotto (n.d.), Ferla (2005/2006), and Maestri (2013/2014). The one dedicated circus building to have been constructed was for Circus Renz in Milan in May 1881, as part of the National Exhibition of Industry, Art and Commerce. As elaborate as it was, it was created from wood. The company arrived in Milan on the 13 May, having left Vienna two days before travelling by train with 46 wagons. 132 horses and other animals completed the travelling stables. The newspaper *Corriera della Sera* of 13 May 1881 gave this report;

La costruzione è tutta in legno, e l'edificio comprende: - Circo ad uso spettacolo; - locale ad uso scuderia con altro superiore per magazzeni e camerini degli artisti; - portico nella parte principale, con atrio e locali annessi laterali, per ufficio d'amministrazione, sale da caffè, ecc, ecc. – Superiormente a questo atrio trovasi una sala per le prove del ballo. Nei fianchi del fabbricato, cioè nei due corpi sporgenti sono le scale di servizio pei secondi e terzi posti. Ai posti riservati, ai palchi, ed ai primi posti si accede dall'atrio. Dodici sono le scale del circo, e sedici le uscite, tutte indipendenti le une dalle altre. di più c'è un'uscita speciale pel re e per la sua famiglia. Il Circo per gli spettacoli è formato da due dodecagoni inscritti l'uno nell'altro – l'uno è della lunghezza di metri 50, l'altro di metri 30. Ad ogni angolo di quest'ultimo s'innalzano 12 colonne principali dell'altezza di metri 16,50 a sostegno del tetto, la cui maggiore altezza è di metri 24. L'altezza poi della parte esterna del circo è di metri 12. La disposizione del Circo è poi stabilita: all'ingiro dell'arena equestre, che misura un diametro di metri 13,50 stanno i posti riservati che si elevano gradatamente in 5 ordini, fino a raggiungere i palchi aperti. Superiormente a questi palchi ne abbiamo una seconda fila e quindi si innalza una gradinata di ben 11 scaglioni, servibili pei secondi e terzi posti. Il circo può contenere circa 5000 persone tutte sedute. L'illuminazione è a gaz ed a luce elettrica. La parte decorativa è semplicissima. Un velario a strisce bianche e celesti con fasce e cordoni gialli e rossi, copre il tetto a guisa di plafond, lasciando scoperte le pareti principali delle capriate, presentando così l'aspetto di un vasto ombrello. Mensole dipinte a trafori di legno ed intagli, capitelli semplicissimi, ma in tutto armonici, completano le decorazioni. Il progetto del Circo è dell'architetto Gaetano Canedi, che ne diresse anche i lavori.

[The construction is entirely made of wood, and the building includes: - Circus arena for performances; - a room used as a stable with another superior for warehouses and artists' dressing rooms; a portico in the main part, with an atrium and side annexes for administration offices, coffee rooms etc. Above the atrium there is a dance rehearsal room. On the sides of the building, that is, in the two protruding wings, are the service stairs for the second and third places. The reserved seats, the boxes, and the first seats are accessed from the atrium.

There are twelve staircases in the circus building, and sixteen exits, all independent from each other. There is also a special exit for the king and his family. The circus amphitheatre for shows is made up of two dodecagons inscribed one inside the other; one is 50 metres long, the other 30 metres. At each corner of the latter rise 12 main columns of the height of 16.5 metres to support the roof, whose maximum height is 24 metres. The height of the outer part of the building is 12 metres.

The layout of the circus is then established: around the equestrian arena, which measures 13.5 metres in diameter, are reserved seats that gradually rise in 5 orders, until they reach the open boxes. Above these boxes there is a second row and a flight of steps of 11 groups rises, which can be used for second and third places. The circus can hold about 5000 people all seated. Lighting is gas and electric light. The decorative part is very simple. A white and blue striped velarium [originally an awning to protect spectators from the sun in open air Roman theatres] with yellow and red bands and cords covers the roof like a plafond [an ornately decorated ceiling], leaving the main walls of the trusses uncovered, thus giving the appearance of a vast umbrella.

Shelves painted with wooden openwork and carvings, with very simple but harmonious capitals complete the decorations. The circus project is by the architect Gaetano Canedi, who also directed the works. *Author's translation*]

The National Exhibition lasted for six months, after which time Circus Renz moved on to Budapest. The circus building in Milan was subsequently demolished.

Across the Mediterranean Sea, Spain had a similar history of travelling circus groups setting up in temporary structures and of theatres that could be quickly converted for circus use. The first real permanent circus building in Madrid can be credited to an Irishman by the name of Thomas Price. Born in 1813, he had been performing with Ducrow's circus in London since the age of thirteen, and became an accomplished vaulter and equestrian. In 1841 he went into partnership with the equestrian Mr. Powell, opening their Circus Royal in Royal Leamington on 3 May 1841;

> Mr. Powell being acknowledged by the profession as the first horseman of the present day and Mr. Price, as vaulter, has surpassed all others; having thrown the unequalled number of 56 summersets [somersaults] in succession ... (*Leamington Spa Courier* 10 April 1841)

The partnership did not last too long because in April 1843 there was an official notice of the dissolution[1] and Price almost immediately went into partnership with an American, Mr. North[2]. This too only lasted for a short period because by 1845, Price is running his own circus. The question has always remained as to why he appears in Madrid, Spain in 1847. An article in *The Era* of 9 February 1845 might give us a clue.

> On Monday night the performance received a temporary interruption by the entrance of Inspector Valentine ... and other officers, who, in virtue of warrants issued ... arrested Mr. and Mrs. Price, the principals, Mr. Samwell and Mr. Rutley, equestrians, and Mr. Bonicker, the clown to the ring ... The whole of the parties quietly submitted to legal authority and were locked up for the night in the station house ... the following morning [they] were taken before Mr. Justice Wightman ... where they were called upon to put in bail to answer informations preferred against them for having music and dancing in an unlicensed house, contrary to the Act George II ... After some

discussion Mr. Justice Wightman consented to accept of Mr. Price's own personal surety for the appearance of his wife, and remanded her husband, Messrs. Samwell, Rutley and Bonicker, to the Queen's Prison, for forty-eight hours, until the sufficiency of the bail could be enquired into. The penalties sued for are said to amount to £500 [approximately £41000 today].

Although the circus did reopen later this incident must have had a profound effect upon Price. The tour did not go well and the weather was against him. By May 1845 there was a notification that the effects of his circus were sold at auction to Carter, the lion-tamer, who took over the management[3]. We cannot say for certain that this prompted his move to Spain but he is next recorded in Madrid working for Paul Laribeau as an equestrian at his circus in the Plaza del Rey. It is probable that Price began to work independently from Laribeau during the 1850s and had his own establishment in Madrid because by 1860 he had also founded the Teatro Circo Price on the site of the old city bullring in Lisbon, Portugal. This was in operation until 1879 when the area was redeveloped for the Avenida de la Libertad. In 1868, a wooden circus building was constructed for Price on the Pasao de Recoletos. Like many circuses of the time this was a many-sided polygonal structure, although appearing circular at first sight. This had a similar appearance to his building in Lisbon, and became the first Teatro Circo Price in Madrid. Price's circus proved very popular, so much so that by 1876 he wanted to create a larger circus. He leased a plot of land in the Plaza del Rey, not far from the former site of Circus Paul Laribeau. The new Circo Price was opened in December 1880. Sadly. Price never saw this as he died suddenly in 1877. The new building was managed by William Parish, Price's son-in-law through his adopted daughter. For a while the building was also known as the 'Parish Circus'.

The internal structure of the building was constructed of iron with stone exterior facings. The frontage to the Plaza del Rey was arabesque in design and bore the title of Circo Teatro de Price. The amphitheatre contained an arena of 13.7 metres in diameter. On the death of William Parish in 1917, the management was taken on by his son Leonard but he died quite young in 1930. The circus went into decline during the 1930s and during the Spanish Civil War the building was extensively damaged in the siege of Madrid. In the post-Civil War period it was renovated and re-opened as a variety theatre and venue for boxing and wrestling competitions, as well as the occasional circus. Becoming more of a music concert venue it continued until 1969, when it was sold and demolished. On the site is now the Ministry of Culture building.

The name Teatro Circo Price still exists today on the Ronda de Atocha in the centre of the city. The Madrid City Council decided that the city needed a permanent circus building and acquired a disused biscuit factory. Construction on the project began in 2002. It opened in 2007 and provides a multi-purpose arts venue with a circus amphitheatre, an exhibition space, offices, and workshops. It is currently home to the annual FIRCO festival (Festival Iberamerican de Circo). The seating capacity when used as an arena is listed as 1642 people. The circular arena has a diameter of 12.9 metres with an external ring diameter of 19.9 metres.

Teatro Circo Price in Madrid, Spain, today (Public domain image)

In eastern Spain, another centre for circus was Barcelona. The circus promoter Gil Vicente Alegria and the former acrobat Arturo Chiesi came together to establish a new circus building for the city. The Circo Ecuestre Barcelonés was opened in the Placa de Catalunya in 1879. Bech (2015:131) gives this description of the Circo;

El circ tenia una cabuda de 3000 espectadors, i el diàmetre aproximat de la sala d'espactles era d'una trenta-sis metres. Al voltant de la pista hi havia cinc línies de cadires, anomenades 'de preferència', collocades sobre plataformes elevades en forma d'escalinata per tal de tenir una bona visibalitat. Darrere de l'última fila estaven situades les llotges, i a continuació dos passadissos, força amplis i separats per un passamans, un per a la concurrència de les llotges i un altre per a l'entrada general. Envoltaven la pista unes columnes des fusta que sostenien la claraboia central. Acquestes columnes tenien dibuixats a la cara interior uns caps de cavall i unes targetes amb el noms d'acròbates famoso, com Léotard i Price. Un cèrcol de llums de gas situat a les esmentades columnes il luminava el local.

[The circus had a capacity of 3000 spectators and the approximate diameter of the amphitheatre was one thirty-six metres. Around the arena were five rows of seats, marked 'preferential', placed on elevated platforms in the form of steps in order to have a good view. To the rear of the last row are located the galleries, and then two passageways, separated by railings, one for the gallery entrance and another for the general entrance. Some wooden columns that support the central skylight surround the arena. These columns have designs of cavalry caps on the inner faces and shields with the names of some famous acrobats, such as Léotard and Price. A circle of gas lights located on the foundations of the columns illuminated the premises. *Author's translation*]

It was also apparently very leaky during the rainy weather and members of the audience in the front row sat under umbrellas! The arena was also able to be flooded in five minutes and water spectacles were presented. In 1883, the first ever 'ice spectacular' was presented in Barcelona. *Le Carnaval sur Glace* featured skaters from the Crystal Palace in London.

The Circo Ecuestre continued in use until 1895, when a programme of urbanisation involved the redevelopment of the Placa de Catalunya and the circus was demolished. It was some years before it was decided to build another permanent circus in the city and in 1919 construction was begun. It took some years to complete and the new Teatro Circo Olympia opened on 4 December 1924. It was a very large and spectacular building. The framework was of iron and it was stone clad. Initially it had been planned to accommodate 6000 spectators but when it was completed it could seat only 5600. A large octagonal cupola, 35 metres in diameter, surmounted the building. This was the second largest cupola in the world at the time, second only to the dome on the Vatican. From the top of the cupola to the ground measured 44 metres. An external gallery surrounded the dome so that in case of an emergency aerial artistes had an available

Circo Ecuestre in Barcelona, Spain c.1881 (City of Barcelona Archives)

exit. A large entrance lobby, decorated with posters for the show, distributed the audience quickly and comfortably to their seats. The circus ring could be transformed very quickly into an aquatic arena, holding 300,000 litres (approximately 66,000 gallons) of water. This was one of the largest of its kind in Europe. Its diameter was 13.5 metres and a depth of 2.5 metres. There was stabling for both horses and exotic animals. There was even a cold room for animals such as polar bears and penguins! It truly was a colossal building.

Always a popular venue for circuses, it did become more used as a cinema and venue for theatre, ballet, and opera in the post was years. Eventually in 1948 the building was demolished. It was said at the time that the iron framework was needed to supplement the post war metal shortage. An interesting aside, although Barcelona did not have a permanent circus after this date the first World Circus Festival was held at the Palau del Esport in 1956.

To the west of the Iberian Peninsula, into Portugal, we have already noted that Thomas Price created the Teatro Circo Price in Lisbon in 1860. Like other such buildings in the region, it was not used solely for circus, but also for musical events, dance, and zarzuelas (a zarzuela being a distinctive Iberian genre of lyric-drama). Some years later, and still existing today, the Coliseu de Recreios was opened on the Rua das Portas de Santo Antao in August 1890. Designed for cultural and recreational use, it was also used by visiting circus companies during its earlier years. It was of an innovative construction for Portugal as the framework was largely of iron lattice. The 50-metre iron dome was constructed in Germany and imported from Berlin. The lantern on top of the dome was eight metres high, one of the tallest in Europe at the time. The roof was also constructed of metal. The outer materials are of mixed masonry and brick, and limestone. The building is constructed on three floors, with the Sala Portugal being the main event space. The amphitheatre is twelve sided and surrounded by seating, above which are two further floors of boxes. There are also a number of 'special' boxes. The current capacity is given as 2846 seated, although the maximum capacity rises to 4000 when the arena is converted to seating for stage performances. After extensive refurbishment in 1994, the Coliseu still hosts many music events and other stage performances.

There were some other notable buildings called 'Circo Teatro' in Portugal. although none were specifically for circus performances. In the north western town of Vigo, the Teatro Circo Tamberlick was opened in October 1882.

Interior of the Coliseu dos Recreios, Lisbon, Portugal (Public domain image)

Taking its name from the Italian opera singer Enrico Tamberlick who appeared on the opening evening, it was modelled on the Teatro Circo Price. It was a relatively small building, only accommodating around 800 people. The arena was thirteen metres in diameter, surrounded by five rows of banked seating with an upper gallery. By 1897 it was being used largely as a cinema and would continue to do so up until its demolition in 1991. The stone façade is preserved and can still be seen today.

Teatro Circo Tamberlick late C19th (Public domain image)

In 1884, the Teatro Circo Saraiva de Carvalho was opened in Figueira da Foz. Between 1884 and 1895 only approximately 25% of the total performances given were circus, reflecting the multi-purpose nature of many of the Teatro Circo venues. Today it is a casino but internally it still has much of the original design. Externally the façade has been completely modernised. Other similar buildings used occasionally for circuses were to be found in Porto and Braga, both of which are still in use.

During the nineteenth century, circus companies criss-crossed the continent and the concept of 'circus' spread across mainland Europe, and then to the north and south. It also spread eastwards into central and eastern Europe. The political map of Europe underwent many boundary changes as larger nations dominated smaller ones, but the circus transcended these and continued to flourish. After World War 2 the north-eastern region of Germany became part of Poland and towns and cities changed their names.

Breslau became Wroclaw and we have already noted that a significant circus building was first erected in the city under the direction of Ernst Renz, when it was known as Breslau. After the death of Renz, it was to be Paul Busch who continued to manage the circus there in the city. But there was another circus constructed in Breslau, earlier in the 1850s. In 1855, Julius Kärger, a property developer, commissioned plans for a stone fronted circus to be built on Nabycinska Street. It was a relatively small building with no pretentious façade, only the word 'Cirkus' above the entrance informed the public as the nature of the building. Initial plans for the circus show a circular arena surrounded by seating arranged into four segments. Each segment was separated by an entrance passage, of which there were four running along the north-south axis and the east-west axis. The arena was surrounded by regularly positioned cast-iron columns which supported the roof, which appears to have been of a canvas material. The whole was topped by a lantern for ventilation and light. The circus opened on 19 February 1856[4] and would continue only for nine years. On 19 July 1865, the only theatre in Breslau was completely destroyed by fire. It was decided at short notice that the circus could be converted into a new theatre and this was carried out very quickly, the new Stadttheater opening on 30 July 1865. After that time the only circus to exist in the city was that of Renz (and later Busch).

Warsaw is the capital city of Poland and there was only one significant circus building in the city during the nineteenth century. There had been an earlier open-roofed wooden structure[5] erected towards the end of the eighteenth century in the city centre area of Chmielna. It was constructed of larch wood and painted yellow. There were two boxes opposite the entrance; the upper for the king and the lower for the orchestra. A shingle roof protected the audience from the weather. Although initially used for animal baiting and other blood sports, the amphitheatre became used for circus entertainments, as seen in the image, from about 1821 onwards. Despite several renovations it was deemed unsafe and eventually demolished in 1852[6]. The building was locally known as 'Heca' and today there is a beer garden and concert hall on the site. In 1882, a stone-built circus was erected on the corner of Ordynacka and Okólnic streets[7]. Initially it was known as the Ciniselli Circus and this implies that it was commissioned by Gaetano Ciniselli, who was responsible for the circus in St. Petersburg, Russia; but more of him later. It was an impressive building, reported to be four storeys in height. The circular amphitheatre was flanked by two 'wings' of buildings and could seat 3000 spectators. It was famous for its aquatic spectacles as the arena could be flooded with water in a short space of time. It later became known as the Staniewski Circus, as the Staniewski (sometimes written Staniewscy) brothers made the building their headquarters. The building continued in use as a circus almost continually until 1939, when the circus was destroyed by German bombing in World War 2. The site was never redeveloped as a circus.

Circus troupes travelled throughout the central European country of Hungary from

Ciniselli/Staniewski Circus, Warsaw, Poland (Late C19th postcard, author's collection)

the late eighteenth century. As early as 1786, the company of Sebastyén Tuschl set up in a small wooden amphitheatre on a site in Pest (the eastern side of the present capital of Budapest) which is now occupied by the St. Stephen's Basilica. Tuschl regularly presented in this structure through until 1796. Later, the company of Alajos Schmidt also presented in the building in 1815. Several companies visited Hungary during the early nineteenth century and it is little surprise that Ernst Renz first brought his company to Budapest in 1857. He proposed the construction of a wooden circus building along the Pest bank of the river Danube (Duna) at a location known as the Dunasor (Danube Row). The building was to be completed by 1863 and would have a 13-metre diameter arena surrounded by four galleries of seating, as well as standing places. The structure appears to have had some form of canvas roof and it was little more than a basic enclosed performance space; it had no box office, lobby, or workshop spaces. Between 1863 and 1866 at least four other circus companies, those of Suhr, Trost, Foureaux, and Ciniselli, operated in the city at various venues, each either constructing a new building or renovating and reusing an existing building.

Renz returned to Budapest in 1868 and commissioned a new circus building on the site of his former premises. This one was designed to have a fixed slate roof and although it was still constructed largely of wood it could accommodate 2000 spectators. The amphitheatre contained both an arena and a stage. In this version of Renz's circus there would be a lobby and box office, as well as stabling for approximately 120 horses. In the same year, Ciniselli put forward plans for his own circus building. His was set within a rectangular building and was not immediately recognisable as a circus. The arena was surrounded by boxes, first- and second-class seats, and a gallery for standing spectators. There was stabling for a small number of horses. So, for a time, there were two rival circus buildings in operation in the city.

As the urbanisation of Budapest developed so too did the development of parks as recreation and amusement areas. The City Park (Városliget) became an attractive venue for visiting showmen and travelling circuses, rather than the Dunasor area near the river as in former times. A zoological garden was also established in the park in 1866 and some circuses used the grounds of the zoo in which to set up their stands. But, by the mid-1880s, the zoo was not the attraction it had once been and it needed a more permanent circus to draw the crowds. Enter onto the scene the circus owner Eduard Wulff (Ede Wulff). He was no stranger to Budapest as he had performed in the city in 1857 with his father's travelling circus. He saw the need for a permanent circus building in the city and in 1887 proposed the erection of such a building near the Eastern Railway Station (Keleti). The city authorities refused this site but the manager of the zoo heard of this and saw an opportunity to locate the building within its grounds. Negotiations were made and plans were proposed. The proposal was initially for a 'temporary iron structured riding hall and stable in the zoo' (Szechenyi 2022:153). A technical report on the proposed structure was submitted by János Rethy in October 1888;

> The main riding hall is a construction of 40 metres in diameter shaped
> like a circle with a forged and rolled iron structure, corrugated iron walls,

fireproof coverage and fire resistant iron staircases. Firstly, the main building consists of 12 iron pillars organized in a circular shape on which the iron structure of the 'tent roof' is placed. This is surrounded by a corridor with a lower roof supported by, on one hand, separate iron pillars and on the other, the main pillars with its binding structure. The main area is directly connected to the foreground which includes the lobby, the cafeteria and the bathrooms. Screws connect the ironwork to iron frames on top of which lays the coverage made of decking and fire resistant tar roof plates. This can be disassembled, removed and assembled again. The tar coverage as a fire resistant material is impeccable, while the decking beneath it is placed in such a distance from flames and the audience that an internal fire could in no case reach it. Moreover, its inner side is made perfectly fireproof through impregnation. The side walls of the inner and outer part of the building are 0.62 mm thick corrugated iron plates which can be removed and put back via separate rings. The roof is secured against one-direction wind and snow pressure with diagonal poles. The horizontal wind pressure on the side walls is balanced by the tight connection between these side wall structures and the other iron structures. The seats are organized in a staircase-like arrangement line by line, beneath them an iron plate undercovering is installed through which space is provided for the clothes of the contributing artists, the tailor's workshop, tools and other things. The side walls and roof of these premises are made of corrugated iron plates without an exception in a way that they prevent any kind of fire hazard. The stairs leading to the 2nd place and the gallery outside the building have their own iron structures, all of which are 1.5 metres wide … The stable is a separate, 50 metres long and 14 metres wide building similarly built of iron, connected by an iron structured corridor and riding hall. It is covered by the same kind of iron roof as the main building, its side walls are constructed of the same corrugated iron plates and the mangers are also covered with iron. The inner lighting is realized with acetylene burners everywhere. Plumbing is installed in the riding hall as well as in the stable. (Szechenyi 2022:154)

The building was constructed in Munich, Germany in 1888 before being transported to Budapest later in that year. The circus opened in June 1889 to an enthusiastic and cheering audience.

Cirkusz Eduard Wulff, Budapest, Hungary c.1901 (Courtesy of Hungarian Circus Art Museum and Archive)

Wulff had signed a contract for seven years to perform in the circus building between May and September. When the building was not in use for the circus the manager of the zoo could use it for other entertainments and exhibitions. At the conclusion of the contract, Wulff was expected to dismantle the building and transport it elsewhere, returning the site to its original condition. However, the cost of such an undertaking were prohibitive for Wulff and it would also have been a great loss to the zoo. An agreement was reached between Wulff and the zoo manager in November 1896 that the circus would be sold to the zoo. In the absence of the Wulff Circus, the building was occasionally used by visiting circus companies and by the zoo. It was not until 1904 that the city authorities requested tenders for the running of the circus building. Matyas Beketow, an equestrian of Russian heritage, became the new leasee of the building, initially for four years on the proviso that he renovate the building at his own expense. The Capital Circus, as it became known, opened on 30 April 1904. As Beketow had met the stipulations of the lease, this was renewed in 1908. Beketow then proposed to relocate the circus building some 80 metres from its original site. This was because the city authorities had taken control of the zoo and wished to return the land upon which Wulff's circus had stood to its original use. Beketow covered the cost of the relocation himself and totally reconstructed the circus. He installed a 3000-litre concrete tank beneath the arena in which crocodiles could be presented. Further buildings were added to the complex and a stone exterior was eventually added.

The building did not weather well and had to be renovated several times until it was hit by bombing during World War 2. It was rebuilt, as the Capital Circus, but continued to suffer from storms and fires until in 1966 it was decided to demolish the old building. A new building was erected on the site and we will follow this story in the next chapter. Through the former states of Czechoslovakia and Yugoslavia there appears to have been no significant circus buildings erected[8], although the circus continued to thrive through travelling groups. It is in the south east European country of Bulgaria that we find a permanent structure. In 1888, a semi-permanent wooden circus was built in the capital Sofia for the troupe of Angelo Pizi. This was in operation until 1892, after which time it was used as a casino. In the ensuing years other temporary wooden structures were built for visiting circus groups but none of these lasted. It would not be until the late 1950s that a new permanent wooden circus was constructed.

To the east of Europe, Imperial Russia produced some remarkable circus buildings during the nineteenth century and the later Soviet era.

Cirkusz Beketow, Budapest, Hungary, early C20th (Courtesy of Hungarian Circus Art Museum and Archive)

Notes

1. *The Era* 23 April 1843

2. *Hereford Times* 20 May 1843

3. *Cambridge Independent Press* 10 May 1845

4. *Schlesische Zeitung* 19 February 1856

5. An image of the Heca can be found at; Dzieje porozbiorowe narodu polskiego ilustrowane T. 2, cz. 1, [1815-1825] - Publication content - Kujawsko-Pomorska Digital Library (umk. pl) p491

6. An image of the Staniewski Circus can be found in; 10 Places You Will Never Visit in Warsaw | Article | Culture.pl

7. Jakobczyk-Gola, A. 2020. *Warsaw Heca; from bestial spectacle to acrobatic arts.* Online at; Warsaw Heca: from bestial spectacle to acrobatic arts (hrabiatytus.pl)

8. Divac, M. et al. 2022. *Circus is a performance but it is also a building – memory of circus buildings in Europe.* City, Territory, and Architecture. P14. Online at; file:///C:/Users/ User/OneDrive/Documents/Opulence%20&%20Ostentation/circus%20buildings%20 PDF%20s40410-022-00156-3.pdf

CHAPTER 9

ЦИРК - IMPERIAL RUSSIA AND THE LATER SOVIET STATES

Whatever our politics or ideologies, it has to be acknowledged that nineteenth century Imperial Russia produced some of the more significant circus buildings of the time. One of the first foreign troupes to arrive in Russia was that of Charles Hughes, the rival to Philip Astley. In 1773, only five years after Astley had begun his venture in London, Hughes performed in St. Petersburg at the court of Catherine the Great; St. Petersburg then being the capital city of Russia.

As early as 1822, in a building constructed for gymnastic exercises on Krestovsky Island, a visiting circus troupe performed, as advertised in the *St. Petersburg Vedemosti* journal;

> On the 22nd and the 23rd of May Rudolf Mex and his Company will introduce different circus ridings, horse racing, dancing on the ropes and beautiful fireworks in the newly arranged building of Iosif Gabit for gym exercises on Krestovsky Island. The beginning of the performance is at 7 o'clock. (Medvedev, 1974:144)

This was a wooden construction, not specifically designed for circus but, however, it is significant in that it incorporated acts other than pure equestrianism. There is no record of the building being used for circus activities beyond this date. Within a few years, the first circus with a full complement of acts to perform in Russia was that of the French equestrian Jacques Tourniaire. In 1827 he commissioned a wooden circus building, called the Cirque Olympique, on a site near the Fontankana canal in St. Petersburg. Designed by the architect Shustov, it was also known as the 'Circus on Simeonovsky Bridge'. The circus was built with a stage and it lasted only one year as it was then bought by the city authorities and converted into a circus-theatre. It survived until 1842 when it was then demolished. It would be another 40 years before a further circus building was constructed in the city.

Carl Magnus Hinné was an Austro-Hungarian equestrian who established his wooden circus building in St. Petersburg in 1867, next to the Mihkailovsky Riding School. The architect was P. Vazuev, and the wooden walls rested upon wooden foundations dug 1.8 metres into the ground. The roof was of wooden boards insulated with thick felt to protect against the weather. The heating of the building was effected with temporary stoves and the whole was illuminated with gas. To assist him in managing the circus, Hinné worked with his brother-in-law Gaetano Ciniselli, a name we have already come across. He also hired Albert Salamonsky, who brought his own equestrian troupe to work with Hinné. The circus became very popular and also very lucrative for Hinné. He retired from circus life in 1875, leaving the circus to Ciniselli. Ciniselli had plans for a larger and more permanent circus in St. Petersburg and he acquired a plot of land, almost on the same site on the Fontankana as Tourniaire's Cirque Olympique, to commission his new circus building. The following description of the building was given in *The Builder* 19 August 1876;

The Ciniselli Circus in St. Petersburg

This building, in course of erection ... is to replace the old wooden structure [the Cirque Olympique] near the Simionoff Bridge, over the Fontankana canal ... The new building is much larger than the old wooden one. It is placed with its principal façade in the Karavannaya Street. Its form is eliptic, the building being surrounded by a row of balustrades. The projecting principal entrance is well adorned, statues being placed in its arches, 16ft. high, and at its sides groups of Atlantes. The frieze bears the inscription 'Circus Ciniselli'. Below the groups of the Atlantes are groups of children supporting the arms of the city. Upon the entrance is placed a group of horses, with the inscription 'Fame to Genius'. The two-storied circus is 60ft. high; the axis of the greater elipse being 156ft. long, and of the smaller one, 96ft. long. A characteristic feature of the new circus is the foyer of the principal entrance, behind the imperial state box. There are eleven rows of seats, and two rows of private boxes. Spacious stables have been provided, as well as ample accommodation in the shape of living-rooms for the attendants and

Ciniselli Circus, St Petersburg, Russia (Late C19th postcard, author's collection)

Interior of the Ciniselli Circus, St Petersburg, Russia, 1878 (Library of Congress)

other employés in the rear part of the building. The contract price of the building is 160,000 roubles (26,000 l.) but further 90,000 roubles (14,625 l.) are required for completely fitting up the circus. Ornamental grounds will be laid out around the building.

The circus was surmounted by a 49.7 metre diameter dome that was supported by the frame of the building, and not by supporting columns. A roof light, or lantern, topped the dome and a three-metre spire finished off the building. This was the first building in Russia to have this construction. The building work was proposed to be completed by 1 September 1876 and was eventually opened on 26 December 1877. It is generally accepted that this was the first stone-built circus in Russia. It still operates today as a circus and also contains a museum of circus. Opened in 1928, the museum was the first of its kind and now houses an extensive display of exhibits, covering three floors. A brief view of the museum can be seen on the Ciniselli Bolshoi State Circus website[1]. Tourniaire had presented his equestrian display in Moscow as early as 1826 but only in a private mansion. It would not be until 1830 that the first wooden circus structure appeared in the city. It was known as the Zagoskin Summer Circus but only lasted for a very short time. In 1853, another wooden structure was built for the French equestrian Laura Bassin, who had married a Russian aristocrat. This, too, only lasted for three seasons. It was Charles Magnus Hinné who erected a more permanent circus

Bolshoi State Circus Ciniselli Museum, St Petersburg (With permission of the Ciniselli Museum)

Bolshoi State Circus Ciniselli Museum, St Petersburg (With permission of the Ciniselli Museum)

Bolshoi State Circus Ciniselli Museum, St Petersburg (With permission of the Ciniselli Museum)

building in 1868, albeit still constructed of wood. Albert Salamonsky assisted Hinné in the running of the circus and although it was popular it never reached the standard of the circus in St. Petersburg. Even when Ciniselli took over the management of both Hinné's circuses in St. Petersburg and Moscow, it was in St. Petersburg that he concentrated his efforts. Salamonsky left the Hinné circus and toured throughout the country before settling in Odessa. The 'old Hinné Circus' in Moscow survived until 1892, when another Italian named Massimiliano Truzzi had the lease on the building. This Truzzi was not the Massimiliano Truzzi who was the student of the juggler Enrico Rastelli. After this time the circus was demolished and a wealthy Muscovite developed the site into a large mansion.

In 1880, Salamonsky returned to Moscow and commissioned a new circus on Tsvetnoy Boulevard, on the opposite bank of the river to Gorky Park. The site was next to the Panorama building, which was a popular amusement place at the time.

Circus Salamonsky, Moscow, Russia c.1900 (Postcard, author's collection)

The new circus was a large twelve-sided polygonal brick building. Around the arena, which had no stage attached, were five rows of seats, a series of private boxes, a Dress Circle, wooden unnumbered benches, and a standing gallery. It was reported to accommodate 4000 people. Behind the circus were stables for 100 horses. Later, in 1892, a large water tank was built beneath the arena so that water spectaculars could be presented. Salamonsky died in 1913 but the building was in almost continuous use until 1985, having survived revolution, nationalisation, and World War 2, after which time a new circus was erected on the site. This still continues today as the Nikulin Moscow Circus, which will be discussed later in this chapter.

The development of the circus in early nineteenth century Russia was heavily influenced by what was happening in western Europe. Hughes, Tourniaire, Hinné, Ciniselli, and later Truzzi, were all born outside of Russia. Only Salamonsky could claim to be of Russian descent, although he did spend a lot of his life out of the country. It was not until the arrival on the circus scene of the Nikitin brothers, Dmitri, Piotr, and Akim that we can see the first truly Russian circus entrepreneurs. Already touring their 'Russian Circus' through the provinces, in 1886 they bought the Panorama building next to the Salamonsky Circus and converted it into a working circus. The building was a natural circular shape and lent itself to easy conversion. Salamonsky bought out the rival company within one season and used it as a riding school and rehearsal space for his own equestrian troupe. He later sold the Panorama building, which still exists today as the Mir Theatre.

Two of the Nikitin brothers returned to Moscow in 1888 and took on the lease of the old Hinné circus. This proved unsuccessful and they moved on to Tiblisi, Georgia, where they erected a wooden circus and made this their headquarters. From Tiblisi they toured the provinces, erecting several circus buildings on their travels. When the building in Tiblisi burned down in 1911, the only brother still working in the circus, Akim, returned to Moscow and commissioned a stone-built circus building on Triumfalnaya Square. It was an impressive building with an imposing façade.

Circus Nikitin, Moscow, Russia c.1905 (Public domain image)

175

The arena had a revolving ring that could be submerged to allow for water spectaculars. It was opened in 1911 and survives today as the Variety Theatre. The original cupola can still be seen behind the new façade of the building.

As Russia became embroiled in World War 1, Moscow had two competing circus buildings in operation, the Nikitin Circus and the Salamonsky Circus which continued in operation after his death in 1913. Akim Nikitin died a few years later in 1917. By 1919, after the Bolshevik Revolution, all circuses in Russia were nationalised. The Salamonsky Circus became known as the First State Circus, and the Nikitin Circus was the Second State Circus. The new Soviet Committee for the Arts invited William Truzzi in 1921 to take on the management of the two Moscow circuses and also the Ciniselli Circus in St. Petersburg (now changed to Leningrad at this time). Truzzi was the Russian born son of Massimiliano Truzzi, of the famous Italian circus company.

The role of the circus now leaned heavily towards a means of propaganda. Lenin, the Soviet leader, once said to his People's Commissar for Education, 'As long as our people remain ignorant and illiterate, the most important arts for us will be the cinema and the circus'[2]. Moscow found that it could no longer sustain two rival circus buildings and, accordingly, Truzzi closed the Nikitin Circus in 1926 and it became the theatre mentioned above. The State College for Circus and Variety Arts, the first ever circus school for artistes, was founded three years after this. The old Salamonsky Circus continued as the only circus in the city, even after Truzzi had died unexpectedly in 1931. The advent of the GosTsirk (Circus Central Management) in 1936, later to become SoyuzGosTsirk (Union of State Circuses) in 1957, brought about a major change. The Salamonsky Circus was redeveloped in 1937 into officially the Moscow State Circus of the Order of Lenin. But the people of Moscow called it either the Moscow State Circus or the Circus on Tsvetnoy Boulevard. It was a new modern edifice in the functional style of many new Soviet buildings. It could seat 1500 spectators and many aspiring circus artistes from the circus school saw this as the epitome of circus.

The post-World War 2 era saw the development of Soviet circus. Across the Soviet Union and other Soviet Bloc countries many circus buildings were constructed. The Soviet Union considered the circus to be very much an entertainment for the masses; entry prices were kept deliberately low and the circus, as an industry, was underpinned by the state, with artistes' salaries and pensions being guaranteed. The biggest development in Moscow was in 1971 when the new futuristic circular circus building was opened in the April. With its distinctive scalloped roof and glass walls, the Bolshoi Circus, or Great Moscow State Circus, is reputed to be the largest circus building in the world, seating almost 3500 people. The circus has five quickly interchangeable arenas, including equestrian, ice, and aquatic. It is situated outside of the city centre, near the University on Vernadsky Avenue. A virtual tour of some aspects of the building can be found online.[3]

Bolshoi Circus, Moscow, Russia 1970s (Public domain image)

The 'old' Salamonsky Circus still remained popular, especially as it was within the city itself. In 1982, the management of the circus was given to the famous Russian clown Yuri Nikulin. To many residents' horror the old building was demolished in 1985 and a new building erected in its place, opening in 1989. The façade of the old building was retained and housed behind a giant glass frontage and the new building was named the Nikulin Circus after his death in 1997. The arena attempts to recapture the aesthetic feel of the old circus and can seat 2000 people. Today, both the Moscow State Circus and the Nikulin Circus are as popular as ever.

Pre-World War 2, Russia had about 50 circus buildings around the country. Most of these were of wooden construction and subject to long term deterioration and fires. In the post war era, especially after the inauguration of the Union of State Circuses in 1957, there was a construction programme in which many permanent circus buildings were constructed over a period of three decades. Many of these still exist, both within Russia itself and in former Soviet Bloc countries, and are in use today. The Union of State Circuses has now been superseded by Rosgostsirk (Russian State Circus Company). The stated mission of Rosgostsirk is to;

> Protect the centuries old traditions of circus business as a phenomenon of the cultural heritage of the Fatherland. Create original innovative performances, attractions and performances. To improve and develop the potential of circus art as an integral part of the great Russian culture[4].

The company is responsible for overseeing the business of 36 stationary circus buildings across the country in the following towns and cities; Astrakhan, St Petersburg, Bryansk, Vladivostok, Volgograd, Voronezh, Yekaterinburg, Ivanovo, Irkutsk, Kemerovo, Kirov, Kislovodsk, Kostroma, Krasnoyarsk, Kursk, Magnitogorsk, Nizhny Novgorod, Nizhny Tagil, Novokuznetsk, Novosibirsk, Omsk, Orenburg, Penza, Perm, Rostov, Ryazan, Samara, Saratov, Sochi, Stavropol, Tver, Tula, Tyumen, Ufa, Chelyabinsk, and Yaroslavl. Architecturally, many of these circus buildings have a distinctive, almost brutal, 'futuristic' exterior design which many have likened to as a 'space ship'. For those who may be particularly interested in Soviet circus buildings, images of all the above-mentioned circuses, with further information on each, can be found online[5].

With the fall of communism in 1989 and the subsequent break-up of the Soviet Bloc, many former Soviet states became independent but still retained circus buildings erected within the Soviet era. In the Ukraine, notwithstanding the current conflict, there are at least five extant Soviet circus buildings of note still in use. In the capital city of Kyiv, the new circus building was opened in November 1960, the previous building having been destroyed during World War 2. In 1998 it became the National Circus of Ukraine. It is situated on Peremohy (Victory) Square. Accommodating 2100 spectators, it has a 22-metre-high dome, and is the largest domed building in the city.

Dnipro, in the eastern region of the Ukraine, has a long circus history dating back to the early part of the twentieth century when Truzzi brought his troupe to perform in the city. A relatively small 'hall' was used for circus until it was demolished in 1929. A new circus building was erected and opened in June 1960 near the Ozerka market. Although it was intended as a permanent structure it had no heating facilities and therefore was used only during the summer months. It was abandoned in 1980 and left derelict when another new circus was constructed. The 'old' Ozerka market building

Kyiv State Circus, Kyiv, Ukraine 1960s (Public domain image)

still stands today but is a derelict shell. When built, it had state of the art technology and facilities for circus performances. Situated in the city centre along the banks of the river Dnieper, it is now referred to as the Dnipropetrovsk State Circus and can accommodate 1900 spectators. Designed by Pavlo Nirinberg, it is typically circular in design with a reinforced concrete roof that has echoes of a circus tent. According to travel writer Megan Starr[6], the building is the only circus in the Ukraine with dedicated spaces for rehearsals and training. It also houses a ballet studio and next to the circus is an accommodation facility for artistes.

The industrial city of Zaporizhia lies in the south east of the Ukraine. Like Dnipro, it has a tradition of circus that goes back to the early twentieth century and a temporary wooden structure was erected as a summer circus. This was destroyed during World War 2 and rebuilt in 1948 with a wood and metal internal frame in 1948. Still only used during the summer, the demand for circus entertainment all year round caused a new circus building to be constructed on Rekordna Street. Construction began in 1966 and the circus was eventually opened in April 1972. Another Soviet styled circular building, it can accommodate 2000 people. It has a small observation superstructure at the top of the domed roof. The arena has the standard 13 metre diameter and the two-tiered audience seating is arranged in eight sectors on either side of the central axis of the arena. At one end of the axis is the artistes' entrance and exit, above which is housed the orchestra. The other end of the axis is the central entrance. Like many other circus buildings, it is also used for music concerts as well as for circus.

The modern circus building in the eastern city of Donetsk has an unusual design. The former wooden structure lasted from 1926 until 1933 when it was destroyed by fire. To replace this a very modern building was constructed, opening in August 1969. Designed by Soviet architects and engineers, it moved away from the more 'traditional' domed style and was built as a cut through cylinder, being higher at the front of the building than at the back. The total diameter of the building is 60 metres and the height is 30 metres to the front. The building has seating for 1850 people.

Kharkiv, in the north east of the country, has perhaps the oldest connection to circus in the Ukraine. There is evidence that a heated wooden circus, later surrounded by brick walls, was set up in the city around 1860. It was used mainly for summer productions. By the late nineteenth century, several other wooden structures were established, one of which belonged to Albert Salamonsky. But it was in 1906 that the first truly permanent brick circus structure appeared. Henry Grikke built a circus-theatre which, after the nationalisation of circuses under the Soviets became known as the Kharkiv State Circus. In the 1930s the building underwent a programme of renovation and the original dome was removed. The 'old' circus still exists today and is used as a rehearsal and training space. Construction of a new building began in 1966 and the circus was opened in April 1974. It can seat approximately 2000 spectators and has facilities for artistes with extensive dressing rooms, rehearsal rooms, a music room, and a conductor's room. There is also stabling for horses and housing for wild animals. The building even boasts a shower facility for the animals. Similar to the Donetsk circus, the Kharkiv circus has no dome. Essentially circular in shape, the glass front elevation appears to lower towards the back of the building but then at the back there is a further cylindrical structure, higher than the front elevation, that lowers towards the front. Then whole creates an almost concave roof line rather than the traditional dome. The Kharkiv circus is still in operation today, notwithstanding the present political situation.

In the former Soviet state of Kazakhstan, the Kazhak Circus first performed in the city of Almaty in 1970, in the old Saratov arena. With the growth of interest in the circus a

Kharkiv State Circus, Kharkiv, Ukraine (Public domain image)

Kazakhstan State Circus (With permission of Megan Starr)

new building was commissioned and this opened in June 1972. The building, designed by Vladimir Katsev to represent a Kazhak nomadic yurt, is circular and domed with an inverted conical lantern at the top.

It can accommodate 2160 people and has facilities for rehearsals and training. There are also two courtyards for the exercising of animals.

In the Republic of Kyrgyzstan, the circus in Bishkek (formerly Pishpek in Soviet times) flourishes today. The futuristic circular building with its fluted surrounding canopy and port-hole style lower windows was opened in 1976. The Bishkek State Circus was designed by architects Segal and Shardin and has undergone several renovations since its opening. The arena can be flooded for aquatic shows and can also be frozen for ice spectaculars.

Another circular Soviet circus building can be seen in the city of Baku in Azerbaijan. This colourful building replaced a series of buildings used for circus dating back to 1890. The Nikitin brothers built the first wooden circus in the city but this was destroyed by fire in 1906, after which time a further circus was erected on the site which also burned down in 1924. A further building was erected and the Baku Circus was formed in 1930 and operated under the Soviet circus nationalisation. The new 2000 seat fully equipped circus building was opened in 1967.

The Tbilisi State Circus in Georgia is unusual in its design for a Soviet era circus. Far removed from the futuristic designs of many Soviet circuses, it is built in a neo-classical design with an eight columned portico behind which are five double door entrances. The building itself is circular with two tiers, topped by a conical dome. It was opened in 1940. The building sits on a hill with a 360-degree view of the city below. After the break-up of the Soviet Union the building fell into disrepair and in 2003 it was eventually bought by a wealthy Georgian tycoon, with plans for renovation. However, it was not until 2011 that the circus reopened. As recently as 2017 the building, land, and adjoining property was advertised for sale with bids starting at $18 million[7].

Chisinau is the capital city of the tiny landlocked state of Moldova, to the east of Romania. After World War 2, Romania was forced to cede land to the USSR and during the Soviet era this area was known as the Moldovan Soviet Socialist State. After the fall of communism, the Moldovan SSR became independent and took its current name of Moldova. The history of the circus in the region dates back to the 1870s, when a circus proprietor named Suru built a wooden circus in Chisinau. This was repurposed as a theatre and eventually burned down in 1875. It was not until 1981 that another circus building was constructed in the city, opening on 25 April 1982. It is a circular building in a typical Soviet modernist style, designed by the architects Shoite and Kiricenko.

It is constructed of reinforced concrete, marble, and granite and has a removable dome for summer performances. The entrance to the building sports a sculptural relief of two grinning acrobatic clowns and there are many colourful reliefs of circus performers throughout the interior of the building.

Chisinau Circus, Moldova 2013 (Courtesy of Darmon Richter)

Opulent stone staircases sweep upwards from either side of the marble floored entrance lobby. The white walled circus arena is the standard 13 metre diameter and is surrounded by tiered seating, with an upper gallery, and can seat 1900 people. I write 'is' because the building still does exist, but it is an advanced state of decay. In 2004

Entrance statuary, Chisinau Circus, Moldova 2013 (Courtesy of Darmon Richter)

Interior of disused Chisinau Circus, Moldova 2013 (Courtesy of Darmon Richter)

performances were ceased and the building was abandoned. The lease on the building was bought in 2008 by an overseas company with a plane for renovation but by 2011 nothing appeared to have been done. The Moldovan government bought back the lease and renovations were planned to begin in 2014. However, due to a serious lack of funding little has been done and the building still lies largely derelict. The Circul din Chisinau (Chisinau Circus) as a company still exists and operates in a scaled down arena of only nine metres diameter for an audience of 300 maximum that has been set up in an administrative area of the building.

The neighbouring country of Romania also has a long history of circus. It was in 1864 that the Italian circus owner Theodor Sidoli first went to the capital Bucharest. He laid the foundations for a stone-built circus but then ran into financial difficulties. The site was purchased by the city and the Athenaeum was constructed in its place. The building was circular, just as Sidoli had planned, and still exists today, although not a circus. In 1888, Sidoli erected a stone circus on Strada Politiei (Police Street) and established his Sidoli Circus there. This building lasted until 1932, after which time it was demolished. Romania became part of the Soviet Union in 1944 but the State Circus was not founded until 1954. It had no permanent home, operating out of a temporary building opposite the National Theatre, so a new building was planned. This was completed by 1960 and opened the following year. It was designed by the architects Porumbescu, Rulea, Bercovici, and Pruncu. It is constructed of primarily reinforced concrete and is circular in shape. The circular roof is fluted and gives the image of a circular 'shell'. The dome, resting on 16 slender pillars, is 60 metres in diameter. Glass walls are set between the pillars so that the circus appears surrounded by glass. The standard 13 metre diameter arena is surrounded by 3500 seats. After the break-up of the Soviet Union, when Romania became an independent country, the circus still flourished. Today the Circul Metropolitan Bucuresti, or Globus Circus as it is also sometimes called, is still popular and the building became designated as an historic building in 2010.

As was mentioned in the previous chapter, in the capital city of Bulgaria, Sofia, a new permanent wooden circus building was constructed in the 1950s. In 1962, a new state circus building was under construction. The building was circular, with a diameter of 37 metres, and an 18.5 metre diameter cupola topped the structure. The amphitheatre included a stage that thrust out into the arena, which had a 13-metre diameter. The total capacity of the amphitheatre was 1800. The material used in the construction was prefabricated metal and fibreboard units bolted together. The space between the external and internal walls was filled with fibreglass for fireproofing, heat and sound insulation. The external of the building was tiled with aluminium slates and glass and the whole covered with a fire-retardant paint. With the opening of the new state circus building, Sofia had two competing circuses until 1968, when the old wooden circus was demolished. A Catholic cathedral now stands on the site. A replica of the Sofia State Circus was built in Warsaw, Poland in 1970. Unfortunately, this lasted for only two years before it was closed over questions of fire security. That building remained empty for some time before being demolished and new housing built on the site. In September 1983, fire broke out in the Sofia circus. Despite the efforts of a small group of artistes and fire service, within an hour it was burned to the ground. After the disaster, a new multipurpose building was planned that could accommodate both circuses and other spectaculars. Design entries were requested as a competition and by the deadline of May 1985 a total of ten projects were submitted. However, the overall project was mysteriously shelved in August 1985 due to 'changes in the programme'[8]. A circus building never materialised, although a tent was placed on the plot in 1987 to celebrate the 90th anniversary of Bulgarian circus. Eventually the site of the former Sofia State Circus was sold to developers in the 1990s and a hotel is now being constructed in its place (Draganov, 2022). Sadly, to date, there is no longer a permanent home for circus in Sofia.

In 1966, the state circus building in Budapest, Hungary was demolished. A new building was planned for the site and the architect was to be Ferenc Barbier. During the construction period, circus performances were given in a nearby 3200-seater tent. The new Capital Circus was constructed of reinforced concrete and glass. The main amphitheatre is circular, with a 46-metre diameter roof that is reminiscent of the circus tent. With no central or peripheral supporting pillars, the amphitheatre space provides an optimal view for all members of the audience. The entrance to the building from the street is a rectangular adjunct that actually hides what lies beyond, and provides an entrance lobby with staircases leading upwards from either side to a gallery that provides audience facilities and entrances to the main amphitheatre.

The Capital Circus was opened on 14 January 1971 and the press described it as;

... a fabulous, glass-made, modern fairy palace; its location remained on the old one in the City Park. The enormous, horizontal rectangular shaped façade is an impressive and up-to-date solution which stands out in the Fun-Fair environment. (*Pesti Musőr* 8 January 1971)

The Nagyzirkus, Budapest, Hungary c.1990 (Author's photograph)

The building has a piped internal heating system so that performances can be given all year round, and at the time of opening it was equipped with the most modern lighting and sound facilities. It can accommodate 1850 people in the audience. Since its opening in 1971, it has been renovated several times but is still in regular use today. Indeed, every two years since 1996 an International Circus Festival has been hosted at the Capital Circus. The latest Festival, and accompanying Circus Conference, was held in January 2022. In 2019, it was proposed to build a new Capital Circus building, to be known as the National Centre for Circus Art, which will incorporate a circus performance space, rehearsal space, an artist training school, a research library, a museum of circus, and public spaces. Until such time as this project is realised, the circus will continue in the Capital Circus building in the City Park, after which time it will be demolished to increase the green space of the adjoining city zoo.

It is now to the west, across the Atlantic Ocean that we turn our attentions.

Notes

1. http://www.circus.spb.ru/en/museum

2. Quoted online *History of Circus: An Art That Paralyzed A Whole Country | 365 Steps* (stepflixentertainment.com)

3. Virtual tour (greatcircus.ru)

4. About the company (circus.ru)

5. https://www.circus.ru/about/affiliates/

6. *11 Soviet Circus Buildings for USSR Architecture Lovers* (meganstarr.com)

7. *Iconic neo-classical Tbilisi Circus building up for sale* (calvertjournal.com)

8. Draganov, D. 2022 *Memories of Sofia State Circus.* Theatre Science Review 45; Circus Buildings in Europe. Hungarian Arts and Innovation Centre

CHAPTER 10

THE NEW WORLD – AND BEYOND

Actually, the 'new world' is something of a misnomer. It was only new in European eyes, as the lands of North America and Australasia were home to indigenous cultures going back thousands of years, long before the European invaders arrived. Imposing their Eurocentric culture on the indigenous populations, it paved the way for the development of circus in those lands.

In 1792, a young man by the name of John Bill Ricketts set sail from England to the newly formed United States of America. An accomplished equestrian, he had learned his art with Charles Hughes at the Royal Circus in London before setting up his own company in the Edinburgh Royal Circus. Arriving in Philadelphia he immediately set about commissioning an open-air amphitheatre on the corner of Market and 12th streets, which could accommodate 800 spectators. The building was opened on 3 April 1793. The site is now marked by an historical marker.

Although there had been other wandering performers who gave demonstrations of 'circus' style activities, equestrianism, juggling, acrobatics etc, this was the first dedicated building in America to house such activities. Ricketts had modelled his amphitheatre on his experiences in England and had, like Astley, created a specific performance space with controlled paying entry. Within a very short space of time, he moved on to New York where, in the July, he erected a similar amphitheatre on Broadway, near the Battery. In the November of the

Historical marker for Rickett's amphitheatre, Philadelphia, USA (Public domain image)

following year a roofed amphitheatre was constructed on the corner of Broadway and Exchange Alley. The interior was lit by a mixture of candles and patent lamps. The building was also heated.

Returning to Philadelphia, which was to become his base for the next few years, he constructed 'Rickett's Art Pantheon and Amphitheatre'. This was almost twice the size of his initial venture in the city and was situated on the corner of Sixth and Chestnut streets. The building was circular with a diameter of 97 feet (29.5 metres) and a height of 50 feet (15.2 metres), topped with a conical roof. It reportedly could seat 1300 people. Internally it was complete with an arena and a stage.

COURT HOUSE, RICKETT'S CIRCUS, AND OELLER'S HOTEL

Rickett's Art Pantheon and Amphitheatre, Philadelphia, USA c. 1795 (Public domain image)

A similar building was later to be constructed in New York in 1797 on Greenwich Street. Between his arrival in Philadelphia in 1792 and 1800, Ricketts set up amphitheatres along the eastern seaboard in Baltimore, Charleston, Boston, Hertford, Albany, and Lancaster. He also constructed a wood and stone-built amphitheatre in Montreal in 1797 and another in Quebec City in 1798.

In December 1799, his amphitheatre in Philadelphia was destroyed by fire. Disheartened, he took a small stud of horses and set sail for the West Indies in 1800 and, after a short stay there, decided to return to England. His ship was lost at sea[1] and although the exact date of the loss is not recorded, his mother registered his death in 1802.

After Ricketts had left America, the circus as a form of entertainment continued to grow on the American continent. Most of them were either presented in semi-permanent wooden structures or in existing theatres that could be easily converted for circus performances. It must be remembered that the use of the all-canvas circus 'tent' was yet to be in common usage. This is credited to the circus proprietor Joshua Purdy Brown who has been recorded as travelling with his canvas structure in 1825. However, as early as 1809 the circus of Pepin and Breschard was presented in a brick-built indoor 'New Circus'[2] on Walnut and Ninth streets in Philadelphia[3]. By 1812 it was being converted to stage more theatrical events and would later officially be designated as the Walnut Street Theatre in 1820, although circus performances were still given, as in this note from a handbill of 1843;

> CIRCUS AT THE WALNUT STREET THEATRE – The manager having made arrangements for a limited period with MR. N. HOWE, the director of the celebrated EQUESTRIAN TROUPE, whose recent unrivalled performances in New York, Boston etc., have elicited so much applause from FASHIONABLE AND OVERFLOWING audiences, respectfully announces that the FIRST GRAND EXHIBITION at the above establishment will take place on SATURDAY EVENING, NOV 4th.
> (*New York Clipper* 15 April 1911)

The Walnut Street Theatre still exists today; the oldest theatre in the United States.

Another well-known circus building in the city in the latter part of the nineteenth century was that of the Philadelphia Circus on the corner of 10th and Callowhill Streets.

The Columbian Gardens in Philadelphia, later to be known as the Tivoli Gardens, also gave equestrian performances and in 1826 it is recorded that equestrian performances were given in the Pavilion Circus in the Gardens[4]. However, in the ensuing years circuses would be presented in either portable canvas tents, semi-permanent wooden structures, and brick/stone buildings. Looking at press advertising for the period, it is not always easy to differentiate between which style of construction was being used.

Walnut Street Theatre (Circus), Philadelphia, USA c.1828 (Free Library of Philadelphia, Print and Picture collection. Castner Scrapbook)

Philadelphia Circus, Philadelphia, USA c.1879 (Public domain image)

For example, the *Daily Alta California* of 19 December 1850 informs us that in San Francisco;

> FOLEY'S CIRCUS – This house will remain closed for a few days in order to allow the proprietor to make some repairs of the exterior of the building.

Later, on the 22 December, it was announced that;

> FOLEY'S CIRCUS – This amphitheatre was re-opened last night having been re-roofed in. Its representations will hereafter be regular.

The use of the words building and amphitheatre might imply that it was a solid building, of either brick or wood. However, the edition of 26 September informed that;

> Mr. Wm. H. Foley has the pleasure of announcing to the San Francisco public, that in catering for their amusement he has erected, fronting on the Plaza, Portsmouth Square, a new theatre and circus, where he proposes producing all the talented, and celebrated artistes in the profession, from time to time, procurable in California.

I strongly suspect that this was a semi-permanent wooden structure rather than a more permanent circus building. Earlier, in August 1850 a rival to Mr. Foley, Mr. Rowe, opened his Olympic Circus but the press coverage for this venture does give us a clue as to the nature of the venue.

> ROWE'S OLYMPIC CIRCUS – The new amphitheatre of Mr. Rowe, in Montgomery Street ... is now completed, and the manager confidently anticipates being able to open on Wednesday next, his company and horses having all arrived. The amphitheatre is very well arranged, upon a much better plan than the old one, the boxes being upon one side and the pit upon the other, and each having separate and distinct entrances. There are also four private boxes for parties, most tastefully arranged; so that the audience, of all classes, can be duly and suitably accommodated. (*Daily Alta California* 13 August 1850)

This seems to be the samsofiae building referred to in the 12 April edition where it was described as 'the M Street theatre', which was being prepared for Rowe and Company. Although not definitive, it does imply that it was more than just a canvas structure and was probably a wooden construction. This idea is supported by the fact that on 28 June 1851 the same newspaper advertised;

> ... a large back ground, 75 feet square, on Montgomery Street, formerly occupied by the circus.

If many of the travelling circus troupes performed in wooden amphitheatres or under canvas, there were those that worked in converted theatres. In 1862, Mr. John Wilson's Grand Mammoth Circus performed in the San Francisco Metropolitan Theatre in an 'elegant amphitheatre, into which this spacious theatre has been converted'[5].

On the eastern side of United States circuses performed predominantly under canvas, or in covered wooden structures. One of the earlier buildings of 'mixed' construction was the Mount Pitt Circus that ran from 1826 to 1829. It was a wooden structure with a brick frontage and was situated on Grand Street. In a 1911 newspaper article[6], Colonel T. Allston Brown wrote that;

> It was remarkable for nothing but its bulk, being calculated to contain from 2000 to 4000 persons. The left wing was occupied in front as a porter-room, and in the rear as a stable. When opened it was known as the 'Lafayette' ... The Mount Pitt Circus was destroyed by fire in August, 1829.

The English circus company of Cooke arrived in Philadelphia in 1836 and a new theatre was constructed for him on the corner of 9th and Chestnut Streets. In his advertising[7], Cooke announced that;

> The interior of the Circus will present a style of Elegant Decorations, combining the extreme of classical neatness and every variety of Magnificent Ornament. The Boxes embellished in a superior manner, with a distinct entrance to this elegant portion of the Circus. The Pit will be found spacious, and will command a distinct and full view of every part of the

Circle. Saloons are attached to the Boxes and Pit, with every accommodation to render the visitors comfortable. The Decorations over the Circle will be of the most superb description, including a Splendid Ceiling, suspended from which a massive Gold Candelabra, the largest in the world, emitting 2500 lights, designed and executed by Mr. J. Foster ... The Circus erected by Mr. Hopper, Builder, from plans and drawings by Mr. Barlow, architect to this establishment. The whole of the Gas Apparatus, Fittings etc. by Messrs. Newton and Whelan.

In 1846, the building was known as the Circus and National Theatre and an announcement in the press gave this description of it;

The Circus and National Theatre will be opened for the winter season ... The whole of the interior has been rendered singularly elegant by a rich classic, light and novel style of Decoration, in which the most gorgeous effects that burnished gold can produce will be chastely heightened by a ground of cream colour and pure white. The Splendid Chandelier (an exhibition in itself) will emit numberless Gas Lights, casting upon the Stage, Arena, and indeed the remotest part of the edifice, alight as cheerful and brilliant as the sun at noon-day. The Furniture is entirely new; the fabrics of the seats and of the reposes are of the best quality; the mats and carpets are of the most brilliant patterns, all purchased in this city. (*New York Clipper* 15 April 1911)

Opulent indeed, but nothing could compare to the theatre that was built at Niblo's Garden in New York. Originally designed by Mr. William Niblo in 1828 as a Pleasure Garden at the corner of Broadway and Prince Street, the site soon incorporated a Saloon and a small theatre. Cooke's Circus performed at the Garden and P.T. Barnum gave his first exhibition there in 1835. The theatre was destroyed by fire in 1846 and rebuilt form opening in 1849. The new theatre could seat around 3200 spectators. It survived until 1872, when once again it was burned down. During its second phase from 1849 to 1872, Niblo's Gardens became a pleasure resort that included the Gardens, Ballroom, Restaurant, Theatre, Concert Hall, and Saloons. It was a fashionable place to be and the theatre offered a wide variety of entertainments, ranging from opera through to circus and variety acts. *Gleason's Pictorial, Boston* of 6 March 1852 described the theatre as having;

... a light and graceful appearance, the interior columns and tier fronts being of iron, and is well finished and tastefully decorated ... There are seats in the whole house for about three thousand persons, and the means of egress are the best of any public saloon in town; all the doors are spacious, and open outward, and the lobbies are roomy and cool. The dimensions of the theatre are – length, one hundred and forty feet, breadth, eighty-four feet; height, inside, forty-five feet.

The same newspaper, in an article the following year on 14 May 1853, gives us more information;

The ceiling of the vestibule, which is supported by richly carved trusses of white and gold, is elaborately ornamented in relief, and richly gilt – the blaze of light being brilliantly reflected back from every salient point. Ascending by four wide and easy steps, the spectator passes into the inner lobby, equally spacious as the last, and beautifully ornamented in fresco paintings with gold moulding. On the left of this lobby are three large, glass, double doors, leading into the interior of the theatre or opera house [or indeed the circus when in performance] – one of the most spacious and complete structures of the kind in America. Throughout the whole building, every seat in the parquette, dress-boxes, upper-circle and balconies is furnished with spial steel springs and hair stuffed cushions, and covered with rich blue damask.

This clearly was opulence and ostentation at its grandest. Little wonder that the writer of the article claimed that;

This celebrated establishment as it now stands, not only holds the first rank among all the places of amusement in New York, but is unequalled by any on the American continent. Indeed it is conceded by many Europeans who have visited all the gay capitals of France, England, Germany, Spain and Italy, that Niblo's Garden, when the whole establishment is taken in to consideration, is unsurpassed even in Europe.

Rebuilt after the fire of 1872, Niblo's Garden continued until the final performance was given in March 1895, after which it was demolished and office buildings constructed on the site.

A rival performance venue in New York, although not on the same grand scale as the Niblo's Garden complex, was that of the Bowery Theatre. The original Bowery Theatre opened in 1826 under the name of the New York Theatre. Its success was short lived because the building was burned down in May 1828. It was quickly rebuilt and re-opened as the Bowery Theatre on 20 August.

Old Bowery Theatre, New York, USA, late C19th (Public domain image)

A lengthy, and somewhat florid, article in the *New York Mirror, and Ladies' Literary Gazette* of 23 August 1828 celebrates the opening.

> The front of the building is covered with a newly invented stucco (of extraordinary durability), in excellent imitation of marble. It is of the Grecian

Doric order, comprehended by a large portico, shown in a colonnade of six detached Doric columns, supporting an entablature and pediment. The porch is attained by seven marble steps ... The width of the portico is fourteen feet ... The exterior of the building is entirely fire-proof, not an inch of wood-work being exposed in any part ... On entering the box-circle, the spectator is dazzled with the blaze of light that suddenly bursts upon him, and it is some time before he can ascertain the particulars of the commingled splendour and beauty ... his attention becomes fixed upon the dome as the most inviting object of beauty. This rises, with a graceful curve, from a circle corresponding to the sweep of the boxes, and in shape is a concave semi-spheroid, very triflingly oblate, the lower part, or edge, overhanging the gallery, as the gallery overhangs the row of boxes neath it ... The ground of the boxes, like that of the dome, is a light blue, edged with a narrow border of white, and surmounted, in elegant and imposing contrast, by the crimson cushions of the fronts. The ornaments, which are exceedingly rich and massive in their appearance, are of imbossed [sic] gold ... The back wall of the boxes is painted of the apple-blossom colour, as being most favourable to display the spectators to advantage ... It can scarcely be necessary to mention that it is situated on the site of the former theatre, in the Bowery, (one of the noblest avenues of our city), between Pump and Bayard Street. It occupies an area of seventy-five feet by two hundred in depth, extending from the Bowery through to Elizabeth Street ...

For all its grand appearance, the Bowery Theatre suffered several fires over the ensuing decades, and was rebuilt each time. Fires occurred in 1830, 1836, and 1845, the latter of which was fully reported in the *New York Daily Tribune* 26 April 1845. Under the management of Englishman Thomas Hamblin (1800-1853), the theatre developed into more of a working-class venue and he often engaged circuses, variety acts, and minstrel shows to appeal to his audience. Due to the fact that the entertainments appealed to the masses rather than to those of a 'high-brow' culture, the Bowery took on the reputation as something of a raucous place during this period. After his death in 1853 the theatre remained in his family for some years but was then taken on in the 1860s by circus proprietor Gilbert Spalding. He made some radical changes to the theatre, creating more space for equestrian acts and hippodramas (large equestrian based dramatic spectaculars). It changed hands again several times before finally burning down in 1929. It was never rebuilt after this date.

Perhaps one of the most well-known circus and variety venues was the New York Hippodrome. Construction began in 1904 and the opening night was on 12 April 1905. The building was steel framed and faced with brick and terra cotta.

It was built under the supervision of Frederick Thompson and Elmer Dundy, who had been responsible for creating the Luna Park amusement park on Coney Island. Compared with other venues of the time it was very large, being able to seat 5300 spectators. The interior was in a Romanesque style, as described here in the *Encyclopaedia Americana*[8];

> The main auditorium was in the Roman style, decorated in Roman red with accents of gold, silver and ivory. "The carpetings are of the same color, and the wall hangings, draperies, and upholstery are executed in a Roman red velvet enriched with heavy gold and silver embroidery and tassels", reported *The Encyclopaedia Americana*. The promenade and lobbies were finished in Caen stone and marble. Off these were the smoking rooms, parlors, waiting rooms and cloak rooms.

Beneath the arena floor was housed an 8000-gallon water tank of clear glass. It was 14 feet in depth and 60 feet in diameter and could be used for water spectaculars, as it was on the opening night when the second part of the programme included horses swimming across the tank as if it was a lake. Throughout its early years it became a venue for a mixture of performances, including circus. In 1923, it was internally remodelled and became a variety (vaudeville) venue and cinema. In 1930 the building was sold to a property developer with the plan to demolish it and build a hotel on the site. This was never realised and the building was boarded up until November 1935 for a six-month period. After this the Hippodrome went 'dark' until 1939, when it was eventually demolished. An office building, aptly named the 'Hippodrome' now stands on the site.

No exploration of circus buildings in New York can go without mentioning the Hippotheatron, which was built on E14th Street in Manhattan on the site of the former Nixon's Alhambra Circus, a wood and canvas structure. The building was opened in February 1864 and then became known as Lent's New York Circus in 1865. It was not until 1869 that it was refurbished and reopened as the Hippotheatron.

New York Hippodrome 1905 (Library of Congress)

Interior view of the New York Hippodrome, early C20th (Library of Congress)

It was, like the Budapest circus, constructed of fireproof corrugated iron sheeting. The roof was of iron, supported by iron clad timber posts, with a dome and cupola of 75 feet in height. The building was 110 feet in diameter with a central arena of 43 feet and 6 inches, larger than that of the original Astley's Amphitheatre in London or the Cirque Napoleon in Paris. Allston Brown (1903) gave this description of the interior arrangements;

There were three distinct places for the auditors - the orchestra seats, dress circle, and the pit, with a wide promenade in the rear, around the entire circle of seats. The orchestra seats were composed of arm sofas, for which seventy-five cents was charged. There were six hundred of these. In the rear was the dress circle, in which there was seating capacity for five hundred persons. The pit could accommodate, comfortably seated, six hundred people. In addition to this, there was standing room in the promenade and other parts of the house capable of accommodating six hundred men, making standing room for fourteen hundred persons, and, when crowded, two thousand could be packed away ... There were two entrances to the building, the chief one being a beautiful portico in the shape of an Italian arch twenty-three feet high and twenty-two feet in width; within was an interior vestibule twelve

Hippotheatron, New York, USA (Public domain image)

feet in depth, with wreathed columns and four niches, in which statues were placed.

In mid-1872, the building was sold to P. T. Barnum who opened his show in the November. Sadly, and tragically for the stabled animals, the building was destroyed by fire on 24 December 1872, never to be rebuilt.

The Bowery Theatre and the Hippodrome mentioned above were typical of the circus venues of the period. By the turn of the century most circuses were performing under canvas but, where they could, they took advantage of the numerous variety theatres around the country. Other buildings were used as necessary and available, as an alternative to tenting stands. Slout (1997) cites several instances of buildings such as Concert Saloons, Academies of Music, Mechanics Institutes, and Atheneum buildings across America also being used to house circuses of the period.

During the middle of the nineteenth century, circus was beginning to make an appearance in Australia, some 10,000 miles to the south. Mark St Leon contends that credit be given to the equestrian Robert Avis Radford for opening the first 'stationary' circus on the continent in Launceston Tasmania in December 1847[9]. However, there is evidence that earlier in Sydney, in 1837, an Italian by the name of Luigi Della Case had put forward plans for an amphitheatre;

SIGNOR DALLE CASE'S AMPHITHEATRE

Workmen are busily employed and digging the foundation of Signor Dalle Case's Royal Amphitheatre at the corner of George and Hunter Streets ... The excavations are considerably advanced, and the upright poles for the framework of the building are already in the ground. The Signor performs with his Company at the Victoria this evening, and will continue to do so for a limited number of nights, until the state of progress of his own establishment shall claim his immediate personal superintendence. (*Sydney Monitor and Commercial Advertiser* 31 October 1837)

This short newspaper insert tells us two important things. Firstly, that some form of planned stationary circus building, as opposed to a short stand canvas structure, was being constructed. Secondly, that other buildings, such as theatres, were equally used for circus style performances at this time. Dalle Case's amphitheatre was certainly on the same site in 1842, as described here;

> The erection is a spacious booth, enclosed within a stout pailing ... The interior is divided into a circus (for horsemanship &c.), a stage, dress circle, and pit – there is no gallery. The fittings up are of the most English style, after the plans of the Olympic, the Prince's Theatre, and the late Astley's – and are without question superior to anything of the kind on this side of the line ... The panels of the dress circle are decorated with medallions, enriched with gold and imitation of trellis work – each presenting a beautiful painting; among these are several Italian landscapes, two Mazeppas, one the passage through the forest, the other the death; and the centre panel is a representation of Ducrow in his celebrated character of the Russian Courier on eight fiery steeds. These are all beautifully executed, and when illuminated with gas from the several elegant brackets surrounding, will afford a coup d'oeil certainly never before witnessed in this colony. (*Sydney Gazette and New South Wales Advertiser (NSW)* 22 January 1842)

Without evidence to the contrary, I strongly suspect that this structure was of wood and roofed either in wood or canvas.

A few years later, in 1850, a publican named John Malcolm opened the Royal Australian Equestrian Circus in the rear yard of the Adelphi Hotel[10]. By 1851, he had erected a more permanent roofed structure capable of accommodating 1000 spectators in side boxes and pit. The building was 54 feet in length by 30 feet wide with a roof height of 41 feet. Over the next three years the structure, now known as Malcolm's Royal Australian Amphitheatre, was refurbished and enlarged to contain three circles of boxes as well as the dress circle and pit. In 1854, Malcolm was forced to sell the property due to ill health, but not before he had again refurbished the building to increase the audience capacity to 1900 and with the addition of a proscenium for dramatic presentations. At the time of the sale, a surveyor's report to the City of Sydney authorities stated that the building was of wood and canvas but in a subsequent letter from Malcom to the city authorities he;

... refutes the charge that the walls are built of wood, having been erected of stone and brick and that the roof is built of combustible material whereas it has been shingled.[11]

Whatever the truth of the situation the Amphitheatre was sold and became the Lyceum Theatre and very few circus style performances were given in the venue after this date.

In Launceston, Tasmania, in what then was called Van Dieman's Land, the 1847 amphitheatre of Radford was refurbished so that in the following year;

It is now a substantial building, securely put together, and properly roofed, enclosing an immense space of ground ... The improvements in the accommodation for both spectators and performers are very great. The circus itself is considerably enlarged. The boxes, as they were before styled by courtesy, are now planned on a scale which will afford an excellent and uninterrupted view of the circus and the stage beyond. Above these, slips will separate the more exceptional portion of the audience; while beneath extends an enlarged and commodious pit. Opposite the performers, a very well contrived stage has been erected on which, as well as in the circus, the equestrian performers will figure ... Beneath the stage are the stalls for the horses, with separate means of access to the stage and the circus, while a sloping moveable platform communicates between the latter. (*The Hobart Town Advertiser (Tas)* 8 Sep 1848)

Researching though the local newspapers of the time there is no mention as to the nature of the construction of the amphitheatre. It was, as stated, a substantial building and after Radford had been declared insolvent in 1851 it continued in use, under the management of Mr. Ashton. Its longevity hints at it being of sound construction but I suspect it was built largely of timber.

During the second half of the nineteenth century and into the twentieth century circuses are recorded in many of the major towns across Australia. However, it would seem that almost all of these were travelling shows that worked either under canvas or in constructed wooden buildings. The companies would also perform in theatre venues where available. This is alluded to in an article entitled *The Equestrian's Child*;

Mr. Condoni's establishment was a very superb one, in fact the most so of any of its kind that ever existed in England, out of the metropolis. He travelled with it from one to another of the great provincial cities, erecting, where he could not have access to the theatres, immense buildings of wood, which often in solidity and splendour seemed more calculated for permanent public structures than the mere portable fabrics of a season ... The circus itself, or place of exhibition, consisted of, first, a large round space, about fifty feet in diameter, depressed towards the centre. From this stretched back on two sides wide tiers of seats for spectators, on a level with the open space for some yards back, but, beyond that, ascending more and more, till the last touched the lofty roof. One of these divisions was named the gallery; the opposite one, which had the seats cushioned and backed, was called the pit. The other two sides were occupied each with a double row of boxes, pierced with two wide curtained entrances for the performers. The fronts of these boxes, as well as the various pillars and supports about the place, were ornamented with medallions and shields, having upon them armorial bearings and paintings, very well executed, of such subjects as 'Mazeppa', horses in a storm, a horse attacked by a lion &c., or perhaps portraits of celebrated race-horses or hunters ... The roof, which was slated, was very high, and concealed on the inside by a ceiling of striped silk of red and white, star shaped, through the centre of which was suspended a very large gasilier, with a profusion of jets perfectly dazzling to the eye. (*The Goulbourne Herald and County of Argyle Advertiser (NSW)* 22 December 1849)

Unlike in Europe, the 'new worlds' of North America and Australasia boasted very few dedicated grand circus buildings. In fact, in New Zealand there is no record of any dedicated circus buildings at all, circuses performing either under canvas or in variety theatres. A trawl through historic New Zealand newspapers and discussions with the Circus Friends Association of New Zealand has provided no evidence of circus buildings. Between the years 1894-1904, the Australian Fitzgerald Brothers' Circus played eight tours through New Zealand, remaining there for up to seven months at a time as they worked the major centres and small towns between Auckland and the Bluff. But all of these performances were under canvas.

Astley's Amphitheatre, Melbourne, Australia c. 1855 (Museums Victoria collections)

One of the earliest circus buildings to be erected in Melbourne was in the mid-1800s and was commonly referred to as the Astley's Amphitheatre on Spring Street. Indeed, it bore that lettering on its roof. Later demolished, the site was used for the construction of the Princess Theatre.

The Fitzgerald Brothers Circus was responsible for erecting a static circus building in Melbourne in 1901, which is now the site of the Melbourne Arts Centre[12]. It was an octagonal shaped building, which they named the Olympic Circus, and could seat 3000 spectators.

A contract for £1000 has been let to Mr. James Moore for the erection of an immense hippodrome. This will be situated on the St. Kilda Road, just over Prince's Bridge ... A second contract has been let to Messrs. Edmiston and O'Neil to light the hippodrome – which, by the way, will be 200 ft. long – in a novel and artistic manner. The approach to the menagerie will be by means of a long corridor, which will be gaily decorated and adorned with ferns, flags, and various kinds of plants. The height in the centre [of the hippodrome] will be 50ft. so as to give the fullest effect to the new and daring aerial acts contained in the programme. The seating accommodation will be especially attended to ... (*Sportsman (Melbourne)* 8 October 1901)

Unfortunately, there is little in the way of the description of the interior of the building, although a news item the following year gave a little more information;

On reaching the show the first thing one notices is the tasteful manner in which the entrance is decorated, this being accomplished by the utilising of numerous varied coloured electric lights. Then we pass on a bit and find ourselves in a large galvanised iron building, and are suddenly startled by the loud roaring of the king of the beasts, who is caged (thank goodness) close by. This reminds us that we are in the menagerie ... We move on again and find ourselves in the main hall, where all the attractive 'turns' of Messrs. Fitzgerald have gathered for the entertainment of their patrons are gone through. (*Sportsman (Melbourne)* 22 October 1902)

It is not entirely clear of what material the main amphitheatre was constructed and there is no mention of it being brick or stone built. It may be that it was predominantly of wood and canvas, or maybe even of galvanised iron, as was the attached menagerie. It was clearly intended as a permanent base for the Fitzgerald Circus when they were not on tour, which they frequently undertook. In the September of 1902 they made a press announcement that they intended to open permanent circuses in Adelaide, Sydney, and Brisbane along the lines of the one they had built in Melbourne[13]. However, certainly in the following year all mention of the Fitzgerald shows in those cities referred to them being under canvas, either in tents or marquees; in Sydney in Belmore Park, in Adelaide on the Old Exhibition Ground, and in Brisbane near the Central Station. There is no reference to 'permanent' circus structures.

One of the few stone-built circus venues in Australia was the Sydney Hippodrome. Opened in April 1916, it was converted from the former Belmore Market building and leased to Wirth's Circus for 21 years.

It could accommodate 3000 people and contained both a stage and central arena. The floor of the ring could be lowered to a depth of 2.4 metres and could be flooded with 900,000 litres (approximately 198,000 gallons) of water for aquatic spectaculars. Beneath the stage and arena was stabling for both horses and exotic animals. *The Evening News (Sydney NSW)* of 3 March 1916 gave this information;

> So far as the auditorium is concerned the audience will have the choice of patronising four portions, the orchestra stalls (to seat 1000), the dress circle (to accommodate over 500), the gallery (to seat over 600), and six boxes. The lighting arrangements are in the hands of the well known electrical engineer, Mr. J. Povah, who is using 30 1/2 miles of wire to feed the 2800 lamps employed ... The scheme of decoration is pleasing and one important feature which has been studied to the full is the 'sighting'. No matter in what part of the building one may be seated a capital view of the stage may be had ... The exits are numerous, the staircases fireproof, and the building, when completed, will certainly fulfil Mr. Philip Wirth's wish that it should be the finest of its type in the world.

The Hippodrome was used for circus and theatre until 1928, when it was refurbished and reopened as a cinema under the name of the Capitol Theatre. In 1933, it was further refurbished and opened as a theatre. In 1999 it was listed on the State Heritage Register of historic buildings. It is the only theatre in Australia to have survived substantially intact. It still operates today as a theatre[14].

In both North America and Australasia there was never the growth of grand and opulent dedicated circus buildings as there was in Europe, although there were a few examples as we have seen. The travelling tented shows tended to predominate or performances (and later the individual performers) gravitated towards existing variety theatre buildings. As to why this should be is hard to define. Both Australia and the United States of America contain vast tracts of land. Major cities were far from each other interspersed with small and relatively isolated townships. While the larger cities could support some form of static circus building, whether it be in an amphitheatre or theatre, that could host a circus company for an extended period of time, the smaller places did not have that luxury. In the beginning, the only way circuses could reach these communities was to take the shows to them and perform short stands under easily transportable canvas structures. And, for all that the circus in these lands grew from a common Eurocentric culture, it grew into forms that had commonality of content but with a distinctly different ethos and aesthetic in both.

Sydney Hippodrome, Sydney, Australia c.1919 (City of Sydney Archives)

Notes

1. Downer, A. (ed.) 1966. *The Memoir of John Durang, American Actor (1785-1816).* University of Pittsburgh Press

2. Walnut Street Theatre -- Philadelphia, PA -- Official Website

3. Berry, C. 2022. *There used to be a Circus here.* Bandwagon; The Journal of the Circus Historical Association. Vol 66. No. 1 p25

4. American Circus Anthology, History of Circus Tents (circushistory.org)

5. *Daily Alta California* 5 November 1862

6. Allston Brown, T. A Complete History of the Amphitheatre and Circus; From its earliest date to 1861. *New York Clipper 25 March 1911*

7. Allston Brown, T. Op. Cit.

8. Quoted in Daytonian in Manhattan: The Lost 1905 New York Hippodrome -- 6th Avenue between 43rd and 44th Streets (daytoninmanhattan.blogspot.com)

9. The St Leons - PennyGaff

10. Lyceum - Magic in Sydney (sydneymagic.net)

11. Unpublished letter. City of Sydney Archives & History Resources; Letter: J. Malcolm addresses the problem of a breach of the Building Act at the Lyceum Theatre, | City of Sydney Archives (nsw.gov.au)

12. Our history | Arts Centre Melbourne

13. *Sportsman (Melbourne)* 17 September 1902

14. Online at; Capitol Theatre

CHAPTER 11

AND THE FUTURE?

During the nineteenth century and into the twentieth century, Eurocentric culture was dominant throughout the world. In this I include the United States of America and Australasia as they both share that common heritage. It was not long before circus troupes from Europe, Australia, and America travelled through central America, the Caribbean, South America, and further into Asia and the Far Eastern lands of China and Japan. The circuses of the Italian Chiarini, the Frenchmen Soullier and Tourniaire, and the American Risley in particular were responsible for introducing the European style of circus to these lands. Chiarini, with his Royal Italian Circus travelled through central Asia in the 1870s and in the mid-1880s he was in Hong Kong, Macao, Korea, the Philippines, and Japan. The circus of Louis Soullier visited China as early as 1854 and also Japan between 1871 and 1874. Risley is always credited as being the first to take a western style circus to Japan in 1864. However, China and Japan in particular had their own indigenous cultures of acrobatics and spectacle dating back several centuries, long before any of the western circuses arrived. When Risley brought the Imperial Japanese Troupe to Europe for the first time in 1866 people were amazed and enthralled at the particular acrobatic and object manipulation skills performed; skills never before seen. Similarly, when the Chinese troupe of Tuck Quy first arrived in England in 1854, they presented physical skills that had a long history within their own culture. Significantly, both in China and Japan early performances were either given at Court or as street entertainments. There were no dedicated buildings constructed to house these activities. When the western circuses arrived, they performed entirely under canvas or in wood and canvas structures. Any existing dedicated circus buildings in China and Japan are post World War 2 and I have reserved research into these for a subsequent publication.

Towards the end of the nineteenth century several factors were to change the demographic nature of the circus audience. The arrival of the cinematograph in the 1890s had a major effect upon the popularity of the circus. Within a relatively short period of time there were many Picture Houses or Picture Palaces established across the country. Hundreds of short films were now being made and shown. By the early part of the twentieth century a significant amount of money was being invested in this new industry. The National Council of Public Morals estimated that half the population of the country went to the cinema at least once a week. For the audience, admission was cheap and there was the security of being in a warm building sheltered from any bad weather. The circus was struggling to compete with this new technological invention but perhaps the most significant competition was to come from the rise of the Music Halls. The Music Halls were not only to attract the audiences away from the circus but it also poached many performers.

In an age of enquiry, the aspiring late Victorian middle classes sought their entertainments elsewhere. It was the more artistic, scientific, and philosophical pursuits that generally attracted their support. They went to the theatre or music recitals; they attended lectures or demonstrations. The appeal of the circus was lessening. Whereas previously it had a democratic appeal across all ages, sexes, and classes the circus was moving towards becoming a 'holiday' entertainment predominantly focused upon children. Whilst still having a popular appeal amongst the working classes, adults were now more inclined to take their children to the circus rather than attend solely by themselves. The circus was losing status as a legitimate art form in itself. Circuses existed solely on the profits from their shows. Any money invested in the circus was due to the circus owners and the profit margins could be quite slim. Sheward & Potier (1990) proposed that circus buildings with an audience capacity outside of the 1300 – 2000 parameter proved to be uneconomic. Therefore, after the end of the nineteenth century, particularly in Britain, no further circus buildings were constructed. Even across Europe, the construction of large circus buildings was slowing down. Was this all due to economics? I would contend that this was only part of the reason. The changing nature of society at the turn of the century, culminating in the events of World War 1 did bring about a significant decline in support for the circus. But there is another factor; the intimacy of the ring. In order to make a profit, circus owners had to attract larger audiences but a larger audience in a larger building creates a 'distancing' effect from the activity in the ring. This is particularly so for the cheaper seats that tend to be at the back of the audience seating and so the intimacy of the ring, that shared communal experience, is lost. Losing that experience, that portion of the audience affected may choose not to visit the circus again, especially if unable to afford the more expensive seats that are nearer the ring. As some circus companies now move towards large scale arena spectaculars, the audience can be overwhelmed by a multitude of sensory stimuli. The intimacy of the ring, 'one of the most universal characteristics of the circus (Jacob, 2018:53) has been lost at the expense of economic profit. Morimura et.al., (2011:12) maintain that, 'the typical audience for this type of show is usually people with a relatively high income that is willing to pay enough to see a high quality show'. In a conversation with Norman Barrett MBE, veteran circus performer and ringmaster, he commented that people are returning to the smaller more 'traditional' circuses because they prefer the intimacy of the ring that allows them to feel part of the 'circus family'. The tenting circus in which he worked, Zippos Circus, has a capacity of 850. Even their static winter show in Hyde Park, London, has a maximum capacity of 1500. I believe that any circus with a capacity of significantly more than 2000 runs the risk of disengaging part of its audience. Only in countries, such as the former Soviet Union, where the state has heavily subsidised the circus, have we seen large circus buildings being constructed well into the twentieth century.

The golden age of the opulent and ostentatious circus building may have passed but new circus buildings are still being created, albeit not solely for circus performance. The Cirque du Soleil has created several permanent sites around the world. There are many circus training schools throughout the world that have permanent bases that incorporate a performance space. FEDEC (the European Federation of Circus Schools)[1] based in Belgium lists over 40 member groups across the world, all dedicated to the development of the circus arts through professional training and performance. Many offer degree level training courses. These schools either use existing historic circus buildings, have repurposed other old buildings that would have otherwise been demolished or redeveloped, or they work in modern dedicated spaces.

The National Centre for Circus Arts (CNAC)[2] in Chalôns-sur-Marne, France works within a renovated nineteenth century circus as well as additional modern premises. Others, such as the National Centre for Circus Arts (NCCA)[3] in London, England work within repurposed nineteenth century buildings. In this case the NCCA has converted a former 1896 electricity substation into a training and performance venue. Likewise, Circomedia[4] in Bristol, England, uses a renovated church in the city centre as a training space and performance venue, as well as another more modern training facility elsewhere in the city. The National Circus School (Ecole National de Cirque)[5] in Montreal, Canada used several historic buildings in the city before moving into purpose-built premises in 2003 in the Cité des arts du Cirque, which it co-founded with the Cirque du Soleil and the En Piste group. Erected in 2004 within the Cité, TOHU is the only circular hall in North America and provides a performance space for contemporary circus, both national and international. It is home to the Montréal Complètement Cirque.

Very recently the Arts Council of Ireland published a report into the study of circus-based buildings which it supports in some capacity[6]. Seven building-based circus organisations were identified in the report, two of which are traditional circuses and the others contemporary circus based. The buildings involved are either privately owned 'sheds' or leased properties. The functionality of the building-based organisations studied focused largely on the need for training/rehearsal/creation space, although two of the report recommendations did address the need for an audience;

> Production standard facilities – with sound, lighting etc – that enable artists to work in high quality performance facilities that allow for test audiences

> Able to accommodate audiences for work in progress sharings

The report also highlighted several European building-based contemporary circus organisations as exemplars of good practice. Notably these included Circo in Helsinki, Finland, which has operated out of a converted gasworks since 2011; La Brèche in Cherbourg, France, which uses a wooden tent-like structure for performance work; and Subtopia in Stockholm, Sweden, which is based in a set of converted buildings in an old lumber yard and is overseen by Cirk Cirkör. In the USA, Circadium and the Philadelphia School for Circus Arts are both based in a 'circus campus' which is housed in a renovated parochial school.

Many of the circus schools have outreach programmes that encourage the development of circus arts at 'grass roots' level. There is a proliferation of youth circus groups across the globe and, like the circus schools, many operate out of their own buildings. An example of this is the Zirkus san Pedro Piccolino[7] in Werl, Germany. Initially working out of a school hall they were gifted a disued post World War 2 military sports gymnasium which, over time, they have refurbished and developed into a training space and flexible 300 seat performance venue, complete with arena space and stage and accompanying facilities.

The Circus Hall, Werl, Germany 2022 (Courtesy of Circus San Pedro Piccolino)

So, we can justifiably say that although the golden age of the dedicated circus building may have passed, there are still many buildings around the world that are used for circuses.

However, there are also some 'new build' dedicated circuses that are worthy of mention. The first is a building project in Uddevalla[8], Sweden that is aimed primarily at circus with young people, and refers to itself as a circus school, but it does provide a permanent circus performance space. It is named Cirkusvarnen[9] and is housed in a former mill and saw mill that was owned by the Swedish circus artiste Reino (Carl-Otto Andersson). Reino and his wife Elsie (also a circus artiste) had a dream to create a permanent circus space within the mill complex. In 2011 Reino died but an association was formed the following year and plans were laid for the development of the project. In 2017 the mill and adjacent buildings were demolished and the building project begun. Cirkusvarnen opened its doors in November 2021.

Circusvarnen in the snow, Uddevalla, Sweden 2022 (Courtesy of Johanna Abrahamsson)

The performance amphitheatre is an octagonal building, with an eleven-metre-high ceiling. Adjoining the performance space is accommodation for guests. The whole of the structure is of wood, in keeping with the traditional style of the former mill. A short film (in Swedish I am afraid) looks at the construction of the performance space and can be viewed on YouTube[10].

In the USA, both the New England Center for Circus Arts in Brattleboro, Vermont and the Madison Circus Space in Madison, Winsconsin are both housed in custom built facilities.

Perhaps the most ambitious and newest of all modern permanent circus buildings is that which is proposed for Budapest, Hungary. A new National Circus Arts Centre is currently in the planning stage; plans made by NCKN Studio with the designer being János Szabó. The futuristic design has been referred to severally as The Miracle Globe, the Magic Dome, the Miracle Sphere, or the Orb of Wonder. From this description it can be deduced that the building will be spherical in shape. It is intended to be;

The Magic Dome, Budapest, Hungary. Artists impression (Courtesy of NCKN Studio)

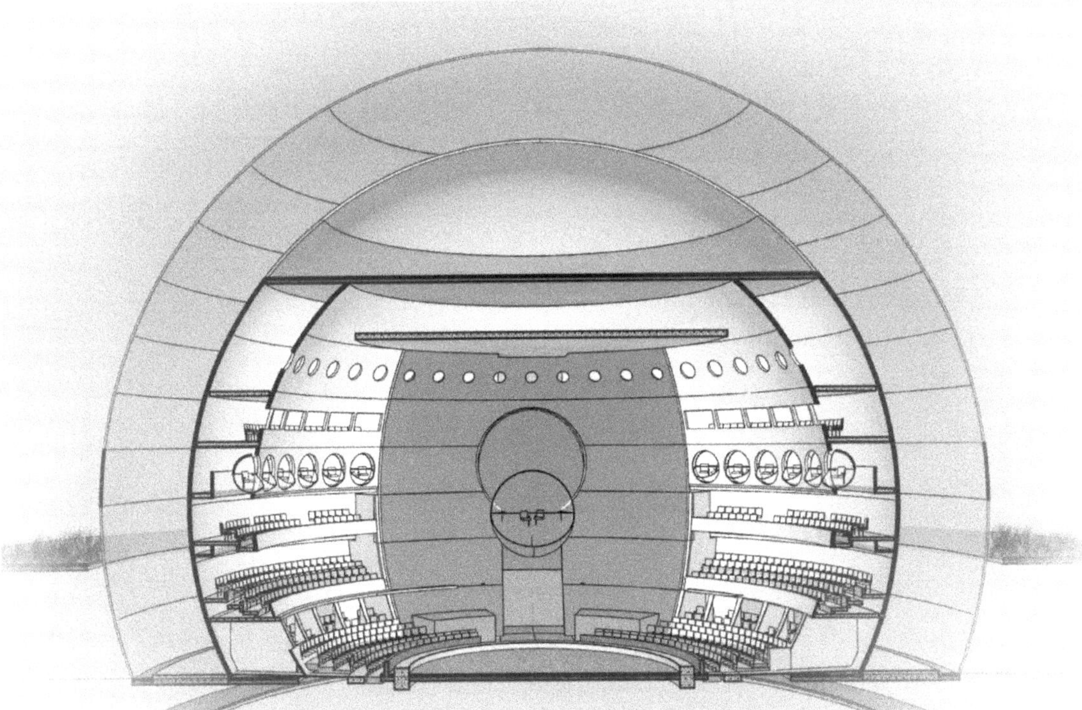

The Magic Dome, Budapest, Hungary. Cross section, artists impression (Courtesy of NCKN Studio)

a magic world enclosed in a glass sphere ... a place of superhuman powers and imaginations ... a cultural and artistic creative space.[11]

It is intended that it should be an emblematic city centre building, highly visible, easily accessible by public transport, and complete with an adjoining hotel for visiting artistes. The building will be fronted by some form of public and event space.

The auditorium will be able to seat 1500 spectators around the arena. There will be VIP boxes at arena level, with three galleries above, and additional private boxes. The spheroid design of the auditorium will allow for a perfect view of the arena from any seat. The upper floors of the new building will provide exhibition spaces, conference rooms, a restaurant, and a viewing terrace making this a building that can be used the whole year round. To the rear of the building will be warehouse and storage facilities, workshops, and a truck park. Beneath the building is planned an underground car park.

In addition to being a performance space, the building will incorporate the Museum of Hungarian Circus Arts, and a research library. It will also include an education and workshop centre for primary and secondary schools, as well as a base for a Circus Arts School; a place where the classic and modern circus will come together for the future of the art form. It will be;

> An arena where experimental and professional work can create together new forms and preserve traditions[12]

It is a very ambitious, and expensive, project which, if implemented, will become the centre for circus arts in central Europe. I look forward to visiting it at some time in the future.

The circus is a survivor. Since its inception over 250 years ago it has weathered many storms; wars, social upheavals, financial crises, and natural disasters – most recently the global Covid pandemic. It is like a rubber ball; squash it and it will be bounce back. It changes and develops; it has to in order to survive – but survive it will. The Circusvarnen project in Sweden and the planned National Circus Arts Centre in Budapest are testament to this.

Notes

1. www.fedec.eu/en

2. www.cnac.fr

3. www.nationalcircus.org.uk

4. www.circomedia.com

5. www.nationalcircusschool.ca

6. *Circus Building Infrastructure*. Report for the Arts Council/An Chomhairle Ealaion. 2022 by Promenade. Online at Circus_Building_Infrastructure_Report.pdf (artscouncil.ie)

7. www.san-pedro-piccolino.de

8. Uddevalla is a small town in the south eastern part of Skaggerak, in the province of Bohuslän, 80 kilometres north of Göteborg

9. www.cirkusvarnen.se

10. (63) Cirkuskvarnen tar form i Grohed - YouTube

11. *National Circus Art Location* (n.d.) Proposal document by NCKN Studio, Budapest.

12. Op.Cit.

GENERAL NOTES

It will be noted that in quoting from original documents, especially newspapers, there often appears random capital letters and uncommon punctuation. These have been transcribed directly from the original sources.

Some readers may be unfamiliar with pre-decimal British currency. Prior to 1971, the pound sterling (£ or sometimes also l.) was divided into twenty shillings (s) and each shilling into twelve pence (d). So, 12d = 1s and 20s = £1. There is another unit that is sometimes mentioned, and that is the Guinea. One Guinea was worth twenty-one shillings.

Conversion of historic currency to approximate current values was made using the National Archives facility at; Currency converter: 1270–2017 (nationalarchives.gov. uk)

For those of you who are not familiar with the old Imperial measures used in Britain for both distance, volume, and weight the following notes may be of use;

12 inches (12 ins.) = 1 foot (ft.) = 0.30 metres
3 feet (3 ft.) = 1 yard (yd.) = 0.91 metres
1760 yards = 1 mile (mi.) = 1.61 kilometres

8 pints (pt.) = 1 gallon (gal.) = 4.55 litres

14 pounds (lbs.) = 1 stone (st.) = 6.35 kilograms

In researching this book, a variety of archives have been consulted, both physically and online;

The National Fairground and Circus Archive. Western Bank Library, Sheffield, S10 2RN, UK and online at; https://www.sheffield.ac.uk/nfca

The National Archive. Kew, Richmond, TW9 4DU, UK and online at; https://nationalarchives.gov.uk

The British Library. 96 Euston Road, London, nW1 2DB, UK and online at https://www.bl.uk

The British Library Newspaper Archive at Boston Spa. Thorpe Arch Park, Wetherby, LS23 7BQ, UK and online at; https://www.britishnewspaperarchive.co.uk

The Bibliothèque Nationale de France in Paris and online at; https://www.bnf.fr/en/gallica-bnf-digital-library

The National Library of Australia digital newspaper archive online at; https://trove.nla.gov.au/newspaper

The Swedish newspaper archive online at; https://tidningar.kb.se

The National Library of New Zealand digital newspaper archive online at; Papers Past | Newspapers Home (natlib.govt.nz)

The Free Library of Philadelphia at; www.freelibrary.org

The Library of Congress at; https://www.loc.gov

-

Every effort has been made by the author to locate the copyright holders of images reproduced within this work.

SELECT BIBLIOGRAPHY

Allston Brown, T. A Complete History of the Amphitheatre and Circus; From its earliest date to 1861. *New York Clipper 25 March 1911*

Allston Brown, T. (1903) *A History of the New York Stage*, Vol. 2, New York: Benjamin Bloom, Inc., pp. 353-356.

Arrighi, G. (2015) *The Fitzgerald Brothers' Circus*. Australian Scholarly Publishing.

Bech I Battle, R. (2015) *La Història del Circ a Barcelona*. Ajuntament de Barcelona

Berry, C. (2022) *There used to be a Circus here*. Bandwagon; The Journal of the Circus Historical Association. Vol 66. No. 1 p25

Berthelsen, H. (2007) *Da Oslo hadde egen sirkusbyning* (When Oslo had its own circus building) in *Byminner* Nr 1. 2007. Oslo Museum Publication

Bouissac, P. (January 2022) The Otherness of Circus Space; When the circus entered history. *International academic conference address Budapest; Circus Buildings in Europe*. Unpublished address transcript.

Brown, R. (2011) Performance, culture, industry in *Performance Perspectives. A Critical Introduction*. Pitches, J. & Popat, S. (eds) (2011). Basingstoke: Palgrave MacMillan

Coxe, A.H. (1951) *A Seat at the Circus*. London: Evans Brothers Ltd

Degeldère, C. & Denis, D. (2003) *Wooden circuses, stone circuses of France*. Artes des 2 Mondes.

Donnet, A (1821) *Architectonographie des Theatres de Paris*. Impr. De P. Didot. Paris

Downer, A. (ed.) (1966) *The Memoir of John Durang, American Actor (1785-1816)*. University of Pittsburg Press.

Draganov, D. (2022) *Memories of Sofia State Circus*. Theatre Science Review 45; Circus Buildings in Europe. Hungarian Arts and Innovation Centre.

Dupavillon, C. (1982) *Architecture du Cirque des Origines a nos Jours*. Edition CEP. Paris

Epnere, I. (2021) *Rigas Cirks; Riga Circus*. Bom Dia Boa Tar

Ferla, F. (2005/2006) *Il Circa a Cremona*. Academic Thesis, University of Milan

Giarola, A. & Serena, A. (n.d.) *Corpo Animali Meraviglie; Le arti circensi a Verona tra Sette e Novecento*. ANSAC Verona

Hills & Thomson, D. (n.d.) *CIRCUS; The Dreamland Trilogy Book 2*. The Dreamland Trust

Hoak, M. (2021) *On the Brink: Circus in the United States & the Spectator Experience of Empathy*. M.A Dissertation. Gallatin School of Individualised Study, New York University

Jacob, P. (2013) *Paris en Piste – Histoire des cirque Parisien*. Edition Ouest-France, Rennes.

Jacob, P. (2018) *The Circus*. Bloomsbury Visual Arts: London

Jenkins, R. (2000) Disenchantment, Enchantment and Re- Enchantment: Max Weber at the Millennium. *Max Weber Studies, Vol. 1, No. 1* (November 2000). Available online at; http://maxweberstudies.org/kcfinder/upload/files/MWSJournal/1.1pdfs/1.1%2011-32.pdf

Kavanagh, K. (2013) Circus is Dead! Long Live Circus! *Unpack the Arts* residency at the Humorologie Festival. 26 October, 2013. Available online: https://www.thecircusdiaries.com/2013/10/26/circus-is-dead-long-live-circus/

Kwint, M. (1994) *Astley's Amphitheatre and the Early Circus in England 1768 – 1830*. PhD Thesis, University of Oxford

Maestri, F. (2013/2014) *Lo Spazio, La Storia, La Cultura; Il Teatro dal Verme*. Academic Thesis, University of Milan

McMillan. S. (2018) *Hengler's Grand Cirque; The Premier Equestrian Circus Company in Victorian Britain*. Vol 1. Smiddy Press. Glasgow.

Medvedev, M. N., 1975. *St Petersburg Circus*. Lenizdat. Leningrad

Ostanevics, M. (2017) *Infill Development in Context; Case Study of Riga Circus Extension*. Academic Thesis, University of Umeå. Online at; Infill Development in Context : Case Study of Riga Circus Extension (diva-portal.org)

Pappalardo, A. (2013/2014) *Il Circo a Catania fra Otto e Novcecento*. Academic Thesis, University of Milan

Radosavlevic, D. (2012) Circus as the Time and Space for Thinking. *Unpack the Arts*, Zagreb Residency Festival Novog Cirkusa, 8-11 Nov. 2012. Available online at; https://www.academia.edu/3819632/Circus-as-the-Time-and-Space-for-Thinking-Unpack-The-Arts-Zagreb-Residency-2012/

Rancière, J. (2009) *The Emancipated Spectator*. Translated from the French by Elliott, G., London: Verso

Schodt, F. (2012) *Professor Risley and the Imperial Japanese Troupe*. Stone Bridge Press, California

Sgotto, M. (n.d.) *La fabbrica delle Meraviglie; Teatro e Spetaccalo n'ell Ottocento a Vercelli*. SEB 27

Sheward, J. & Potier, D. (1990) *97 Years of Blackpool Tower Circus*. Circus Friends Association

Slout, W. (1997) *Clowns and Cannons; The American circus during the Civil War*. Emeritus Enterprise Book. California

Smollett, T. (1983) *The Expedition of Humphrey Clinker*. Penguin, London

Speaight, G. (1980) *A History of the Circus*. Tantivy Press. London

St Leon, M. (2011) *Circus; The Australian Story*. Melbourne books

Stoddart, H. (2000) *Rings of Desire, Circus history and representation*. Manchester: Manchester University Press

Strandner, L. (2008) *Lorensbergs Cirkus 1884 - 1969*. Klädesholmen

Sysoeva, E. & Trushina, E. (n.d.) *Constructive singularities and energy efficiency of St Petersburg historic circuses*. IOP Conf. Ser: Earth Environ. Sci 90 012090

Szechenyi, M. (2022) *The story of the origins, construction and selling of the Wulff Circus in Budapest 1889-1896*. Theatre Science Review 45; Circus Buildings in Europe. Hungarian Arts and Innovation Centre.

Truman, R. (2018) *Aerialist. The colourful life of a trapeze artist*. (n.p.): Author

Turner, J. (2001) *Historical Hengler's Circus 1877 – 1882*. Lingdale Press. Liverpool

Ward. S. (2021) *The Victorian Circuses of Leeds*. Amazon

Willson Disher, M. 1937 *Greatest Show on Earth*. G. Bell and Sons. London

ABOUT THE AUTHOR

Steve Ward has a background in theatre and clowning. Moving into teaching he soon recognised that as well as an artistic activity, circus could play an important role in the educational and social development of young people. From his early days in experimenting with circus in the classroom, and projects linking the professional circus, schools, and youth groups he went on to run his own award-winning youth circus, as well as establishing the original National Association of Youth Circus in the UK. Steve has created and directed many youth circus festivals in the UK, as well as in Germany and Brazil. With a deep-rooted interest in the circus, he now writes about its fascinating cultural history. He has a PhD by Published Works in Social History from the University of Hull, and is a member of the Circus Research Network and the Circus Arts Research Platform, both international organisations. To date, he has written seven books and many articles on the subject. Steve also lectures on aspects of circus history, notably at the first International Academic Conference on Circus Buildings in Budapest in 2022, and has appeared on television and in many radio interviews in connection with the subject. He also advises on educational and youth circus matters – and he still finds time to occasionally perform as a clown!

His previous Circus publications are;

- *Beneath the Big Top; A Social History of the Circus in Britain*   Pen & Sword 2014
- *Sawdust Sisterhood; How Circus Empowered Women*   Fonthill Media 2016
- *Circus Notes & Jottings*   Amazon 2017
- *Father of the Modern Circus; Billy Buttons; The Life & Times of Philip Astley*   Pen & Sword 2018
- *Nineteenth Century Circus Poster Art*   Amazon 2018

- *The Victorian Circuses of Leeds; A guided walk* Amazon 2021
- *Artistes of Colour; Ethnic Diversity and Representation in the Victorian Circus* Modern Vaudeville Press 2021 (long-listed for the Society of Theatre Research book award 2022)

Other books by Steve Ward;

-*Robin's Wood*   Createspace Publishing Platform 2013

- *The Indentured Man*   Createspace Publishing Platform 2014

- *Tales from the Big House; Temple Newsam*   Pen & Sword 2017

- *The Boy with the Flame Coloured Hair* Amazon 2021

INDEX

OTHER BOOKS BY MODERN VAUDEVILLE PRESS

Juggling: Or How to Become a Juggler (annotated edition)

Rupert Ingalese, annotated by Thom Wall
ISBN – 978-1733971201
99 pages
MSRP: $15 USD

The fully annotated edition of Rupert Ingalese's 1921 "how to juggle" manual. This book covers basic juggling technique, tricks with hats and canes, practice methodology, and more. Ingalese's manuscript provides an interesting look at the state of juggling pedagogy in Britain's music hall era. Annotations by juggler and circus researcher Thom Wall bring insight and context to Ingalese's descriptions and instructions.

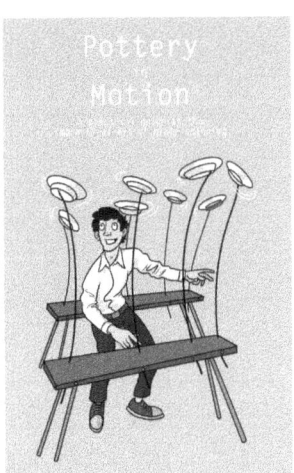

Pottery in Motion

Sam Veale
ISBN – 978-1733971232
71 pages
MSRP: $15 USD

British juggler Sam Veale's *Pottery in Motion* is the first of its kind - a straightforward book that provides aspiring plate spinners both the specifics of the props (such as plates, sticks, and rack) and comprehensive instruction on the skill of plate spinning itself. This small but detail-packed guide appeals to individuals looking to learn plate spinning and provides the knowledge to take it to a performance-ready level, just add practice.

Juggling: From Antiquity to the Middle Ages

Thom Wall
ISBN – 978-0578410845
129 pages
MSRP: $25 USD

As with dance, so with juggling—the moment that the performer finishes the routine, their act ceases to exist beyond the memory of the audience. There is no permanent record of what transpired, so studying the ancient roots of juggling is fraught with difficulty. Using the records that do exist, juggling appears to have emerged around the world in cultures independent of one another in the ancient past. Paintings in Egypt from 2000 BCE show jugglers engaged in performance. Stories from the island nation of Tonga place juggling's creation with their goddess of the underworld—a figure who has guarded a cave since time immemorial. Juggling games and rituals are pervasive in isolated Inuit cultures in northern Canada and Greenland. Though the earliest representation of juggling is 4,000 years old, the practice is surely much older—in the same way that humans were doubtlessly singing and dancing long before the first bone flute was created.

This book is an attempt to catalogue this tangible history of juggling in human culture. It is the story of juggling, represented in art and writing from around the world, across time. Although much has been written about modern jugglers–specific performers, their props, and their routines–little has been said about those who first developed the craft. As juggling enters a golden age in the internet era, *Juggling: From Antiquity to the Middle Ages* offers a look into the past—to the origins of our art form.

Spanish Edition:

Malabares - desde la Antigüedad hasta la Edad Media: la historia olvidada de lanzar y cachar

Thom Wall, et. al.
ISBN – 978-1733971263
179 pages
MSRP: $25 USD

Malabares - desde Antigüedad hasta la Edad Media, es un divertido viaje por países, por épocas. Desde el Antiguo Egipto y sus ya famosas malabaristas profesionales de la tumba nº 15 de Beni Hasan, a los juegos para niñas de la isla de Tonga y otras zonas del Pacífico Sur; pasando por los edictos del rey Alfonso X de Castilla sobre la regulación de los juglares o los antipodistas aztecas actuando ante el Papa Clemente VII en el siglo XVI. También reserva un espacio al final del libro para, aprovechando su faceta de lingüista, realizar unas reflexiones acerca de la propia definición de la palabra "juggling"[malabarismo] a lo largo del tiempo y sus orígenes. Es, por tanto, un libro ideal no solo para malabaristas o cirqueros, sino para cualquiera con curiosidad sobre la historia, en especial de aquellos hechos que en ocasiones pasan más desapercibidos en los textos cotidianos.

A través de este libro aprendemos sobre leyendas y juegos antiguos, fantaseamos con grandes artistas y actuaciones que nunca podremos ver y que nos hacen dudar sobre esa tan manida sentencia que a veces afirma "esto nunca se ha hecho antes". *-Malabares en su Tinta*

Juggling: What It Is and How to Do It

Thom Wall, et. al.
ISBN – 978-1-7339712-5-6
224 pages
MSRP: $25 USD

Juggling: What It Is and How to Do It teaches learners of all ages how to juggle – one of the world's oldest artforms. With a kind demeanor, humor, and enthusiasm, this authoritative manual explains the process of juggling through four different modalities, bolstered by the latest physical education research.

Juggling is an accessible primer that a middle-schooler can hit the ground running with, or that families can enjoy together. The result of six years of work by 2021 International Jugglers' Association *Excellence in Education* award winner and former Cirque du Soleil juggler Thom Wall and featuring guest chapters by some of today's juggling masters, *Juggling* provides great content for even the most serious adult learner.

Book plus Juggling Kit!
Includes juggling balls by Alchemy Juggling

MSRP: $60 USD

This exclusive kit makes the perfect gift for any aspiring juggler. Includes one copy of *Juggling: What It Is and How to Do It* and three professional-grade beanbags.

Beanbag specs: 90g ea., approx. 2.75" diameter. Machine washable / dryable. Made in USA.

Body Talk: Basic Mime

Mario Diamond
ISBN – 978-1733971218
73 pages
MSRP: $15 USD

Body Talk: Basic Mime covers the fundamental skills of mime in an easily accessible workbook format. Diamond brings over 40 years of teaching and performance experience to *Body Talk*, which includes rich photography illustrating various mime techniques.

"[*Body Talk: Basic Mime*] should be required reading for any theater participant looking to incorporate elements of mime into their routines." - *Midwest Book Review*

French Edition:
Corps Expressif: Base du Mime

Mario Diamond
ISBN – 978-1958604984
68 pages
MSRP: $15 USD

Mario a écrit un tour de force sur l'art du mime. Ce livre est éloquent et concis... riche en outils pour les élèves comme pour les professeurs, facile à comprendre et rempli d'exercices pratiques. Ce livre est brodé de segments historiques et anecdotiques qui en font un manuscrit amusant, plein d'observations charmantes et bouffonnes qui font de Mario un artiste phénoménal, prodigue de la caractéristique définitive du mime, la personnalité.

Circus Games (v1.1)

Compiled by Lucy Little & the American Youth Circus Organization (AYCO)
ISBN – 9781733971225
124 pages
MSRP: $15 USD

With over 100 games organized for optimal use in cooperative movement based settings, this is a must have for every circus school, teaching artist, and arts education program! Games are organized by age, number of participants, energy level, and social/emotional learning outcome, and also includes special notes for working with a variety of populations that may require adaptation or modifications to each game. Find more info about the project here:
https://www.americancircuseducators.org/gamesproject/

The ABC Tour

Jon Udry
ISBN - 978-0578410852
MSRP: $25 USD

Ever felt like a challenge? For juggler and comedian, Jon Udry, the ABC Tour — 26 letters, 26 shows — seems the perfect way to shake things up.

What started as a silly idea he believed would take two to three months to complete, ended up being a mammoth three year project that included some of the toughest, most brutal and most enjoyable performances of his life.

From attempting to juggle while wearing roller skates and the unexpected discoveries of performing at a Naturist's Resort, to the challenges that came with working in rainforest conditions covered in ants or in snowy conditions at -10°C, Jon tells the full story from A to Z.

Circus Training Journal

Thom Wall & Rebecca Starr,
Consultant editor: Sarah Baker
ISBN – 978-1-7339712-9-4
9×6" paperback
380 pages
MSRP: $20 USD

What's measured is managed! The *Circus Training Journal* is the result of a year of collaboration between Thom Wall and Rebecca Starr, head aerial coach at Circadium: School of Contemporary Circus. This undated journal, spanning three months of daily training, tracks workouts, nutrition, goal-setting, and more. Heavyweight groundwood paper optimized for ballpoint and pencil.

Mongolian Contortion: An Ethnographic Inquiry (monograph)

Mariam Ala-Rashi
Monograph / no ISBN
100 pages
MSRP: $10 USD (eBook)

This project introduces the performance art form of Mongolian contortion by examining its theories and functions before and after the establishment of the Mongolian State Circus in 1941. Through qualitative research it investigates events that led to the transformation and re-emergence of Traditional Mongolian Contortion in Mongolia as an international export to the West in recent years. Mongolian Contortion examines the numerous challenges contortionists face with traditional aesthetics and presentations, and proposes solutions for the safeguarding of this art form.

Chinese Contortion (monograph)

Mariam Ala-Rashi
Monograph / no ISBN
138 pages
MSRP: $10 USD (eBook)

China's Bending Bodies:
Contortionists and Politics in China
Mariam Ala-Rashi

This research study proposes an introduction to the performance art form *contortionism* by examining its theories and functions throughout the 20th and 21st century. It considers themes including the appropriation of contortionism during the golden age of Hollywood and discusses definition issues between contortionism and other disciplines that highlight body flexibility, such as gymnastics and yoga. By examining the genesis of contortionism in ancient China, it aims to explore parallels between the origins of Chinese contortionism and the establishment of Chinese acrobatics. It later dissects the political use of contortionism in socialist China and the development and institutionalization of acrobatic troupes since the founding of the People's Republic of China in 1949. Drawing upon a Foucauldian perspective, it further examines the parallels between the Western training of soldiers during the 17th and 18th century, and methods of traditional Chinese acrobatic training in the 21st century at the *Beijing International Art School*. This monograph includes data from a wide range of literature, material evidence, oral history, current media reports, and considers recent work in anthropology, archaeology, and political history. It, therefore, offers the interested reader, the scholar, the contortionist and contortion practitioner a substantial treatise about the art-form *contortionism*.

Artistes of Colour

Steve Ward, PhD
ISBN – 978-1-7339712-7-0
317 pages
MSRP: $25 USD

In a society that places an increasing value in ethnic diversity and cultural identity, the contribution that performers from a variety of ethnic backgrounds made to the development of the circus in the nineteenth century is often dismissed and largely forgotten. Using contemporary records and images, *Artistes of Colour* explores the wealth and depth of talented black and other performers of colour, and the contribution they made to the success of the nineteenth century circus. Ward draws iconic figures from the margins of history and gives them the recognition they deserve, illustrating what the BBC calls "a field of study that has been overlooked far too long."

Long-listed for the American Society for Theatre Research 2022 Book Award.

Coming Soon:

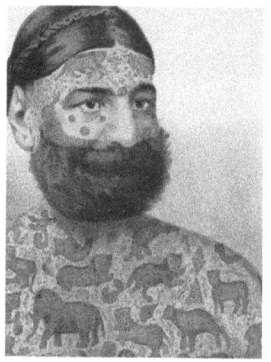

Captain George

Amelia Osterud, Edited by Fritz Grobe
MSRP: $25 USD
Coming in 2024!

    The life and times of the world's most celebrated illustrated man.

The Contemporary Circus Handbook: A guide to creating, funding, producing, organizing and touring shows for the 21st century

Eric Bates
ISBN – 978-1-958604-03-8
MSRP: $25 USD
Coming July 2023!

    The Contemporary Circus Handbook contains interviews with more than 25 professionals, from Gypsy Snider of the celebrated contemporary circus company "The Seven Fingers" to Lydia Bouchard of La Resistance about their work in the performing arts world. Combining Eric Bates' (Cie Barcode, Cirque du Soleil, et. al.) hard won wisdom as well as tips and insights from his contemporaries, what emerges is an invaluable blueprint of how to progress from the seed of an idea for a show to the full touring timeline. The scope of the book is wide but deeply hands-on, diving into practical details on how to find an agent, start your own company, secure funding and build your niche brand. *The Contemporary Circus Handbook* truly is a unique offering to the circus world, full of insider tips and years of accumulated knowledge from industry insiders.

Artistes of Colour

Steve Ward, PhD
ISBN – 978-1-7339712-7-0
317 pages
MSRP: $25 USD

In a society that places an increasing value in ethnic diversity and cultural identity, the contribution that performers from a variety of ethnic backgrounds made to the development of the circus in the nineteenth century is often dismissed and largely forgotten. Using contemporary records and images, *Artistes of Colour* explores the wealth and depth of talented black and other performers of colour, and the contribution they made to the success of the nineteenth century circus. Ward draws iconic figures from the margins of history and gives them the recognition they deserve, illustrating what the BBC calls "a field of study that has been overlooked far too long."

Long-listed for the American Society for Theatre Research 2022 Book Award.

Coming Soon:

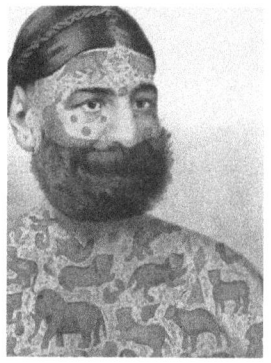

Captain George

Amelia Osterud, Edited by Fritz Grobe
MSRP: $25 USD
Coming in 2024!

The life and times of the world's most celebrated illustrated man.

The Contemporary Circus Handbook: A guide to creating, funding, producing, organizing and touring shows for the 21st century

Eric Bates
ISBN – 978-1-958604-03-8
MSRP: $25 USD
Coming July 2023!

The Contemporary Circus Handbook contains interviews with more than 25 professionals, from Gypsy Snider of the celebrated contemporary circus company "The Seven Fingers" to Lydia Bouchard of La Resistance about their work in the performing arts world. Combining Eric Bates' (Cie Barcode, Cirque du Soleil, et. al.) hard won wisdom as well as tips and insights from his contemporaries, what emerges is an invaluable blueprint of how to progress from the seed of an idea for a show to the full touring timeline. The scope of the book is wide but deeply hands-on, diving into practical details on how to find an agent, start your own company, secure funding and build your niche brand. *The Contemporary Circus Handbook* truly is a unique offering to the circus world, full of insider tips and years of accumulated knowledge from industry insiders.

The Kakubei Jishi
The Rise, Fall, and Restoration of a Japanese Folk Performing Art

Mariam Ala-Rashi

Kakubei Jishi: The Rise, Fall, and Restoration of a Japanese Folk Performing Art (monograph)

Mariam Ala-Rashi
MSRP: $10 USD (eBook)
Coming June 2023!

The art of Kakubei Jishi is a lion dance that is exclusive to Japan's Niigata prefecture, originating in the village of Tsukigata. It is an acrobatic dance performed by children wearing wooden lion masks on top of their heads.

Starting with the analysis of the origin stories of the Kakubei Jishi and the developments of street performances during the Edo period (1603-1867), this work explores the art-form's Meiji era downfall and its subsequent revival in the 20th century.

The Kakubei Jishi lion dance community today is troubled by decreasing birth rates, a drastic decline in the Japanese population and urban migration, and proposes solutions for the safeguarding of this art form. As of June 2022, only seven children are left to continue the tradition of Kakubei Jishi performances. As more and more young families move away from the village and into bigger cities, the future of the Kakubei Jishi is uncertain. It is currently expected that only four performers will continue their training for the 2023 performance: the bare minimum needed for a performance.

Contortion and Practices of Body Flexibility in East Asia - Mongolia, China, Japan

Mariam Ala-Rashi
MSRP: $25 USD
Coming June 2023!

This compendium includes three studies that examine contortion and practices of body flexibility in East Asia: China, Mongolia and Japan. It explores the performance art forms of Chinese contortion, Mongolian contortion and Japan's Kakubei Jishi lion dance of the Niigata prefecture.

These studies investigate the history and genesis of these art forms, illuminating how they developed in various political and social climates. This work further examines artists' training processes, their training environment, the development of aesthetics, symbolism in costuming and body movements, religious themes, mythology and natural phenomena, and costume designs.

This compendium includes data from a wide range of literature, material evidence, oral history, contemporary media reports, and considers recent work in anthropology, archaeology, and political history. A great fit for any interested reader, scholar, contortionist and contortion practitioner who's looking for a substantial treatise about contortionism and practices of body flexibility.

The Century's Juggler

Reinhold Batburger, translated by Kathrin Wagner, edited by Thom Wall
MSRP: $25 USD
Coming in 2024!

He throws a ball in the air and makes millions. And millions of people watch – and did for more than fifty years.

His performance takes seven minutes, and that's his life. Reinhold Batberger tells a family story – the story of a world career, the story of the life and art of juggler Francis Brunn (1922-2004).

www.ingramcontent.com/pod-product-compliance
Lightning Source LLC
Chambersburg PA
CBHW041509120626
46551CB00018B/2360